MENTAL
TOUGHNESS
FOR
GOLF

THE MINDS OF WINNERS

MENTAL
TOUGHNESS
FOR
GOLF
THE MINDS OF WINNERS

Dr Brian Hemmings
Dr Hugh Mantle OBE
Jeremy Ellwood

FOREWORD BY
Colin Montgomerie OBE

This edition first published in the UK in 2007
By Green Umbrella Publishing

© Green Umbrella Publishing 2007

Publishers: Jules Gammond and Vanessa Gardner

Creative Director: Kevin Gardner

Picture Credits: Getty Images

Printed and bound by Butler and Tanner

ISBN: 978-1-906229-15-3

Acknowledgements

We would like to thank all the individuals who gave up their time to be interviewed about their personal experiences in golf, and consented for their stories to be included in this book. In particular we thank them for their openness and honesty in talking about issues that may help those who read this set of stories. We also thank the many people behind the scenes who assisted in arranging or transcribing the interviews.

Contents

Foreword

We've probably all heard someone say that golf is 90% mental and only 10% physical. This book's series of real life experiences clearly highlights why there's much truth in that statement. The winners' stories presented here demonstrate that whatever their circumstances, mentally strong players are able to produce positive outcomes, often against all odds.

The authors have successfully sought out first-hand evidence from professional and elite amateur players, with the resulting dialogues encapsulating all that is good in preparation. They then elaborate and reflect on those attitudes that form the bedrock of mental toughness.

The good news is there's absolutely no reason why any golfer – whatever their standard – cannot benefit from the insights unearthed in this book. The stories provide potent evidence of the power of the mind.

All three authors are passionate about improving the performance of every golfer. Through their interviews they have uncovered the critical psychological factors that make winners – factors accessible to all players. These fascinating stories, relayed through the players' own words, represent a refreshing way to guide, inform and expand our mental approaches to performance.

The authors are experts in this field and should be commended for providing an easy-to-read and understandable book, rather than indulging in abstract principles, terms and concepts. The experiences of mental toughness told in these pages will prove an important stepping stone towards wider acceptance of the value of developing a better mental approach to golf – an area of performance preparation all too often neglected by the majority of players.

There's a well-known phrase that says, "if we do not change direction then we are likely to end up with what we always had." In many cases what we 'always had' was poor performance resulting in emotional dissatisfaction. This book can help you change the way you think about the mental side of golf, while simultaneously providing you with a highly enjoyable read.

Colin Montgomerie OBE

Introduction

Nobody arrives on tour or in the upper realms of amateur golf without being able to hit the ball well. What determines who progresses to the next level, and who flatters only to deceive, is often what goes on between the ears. "Ninety percent of golf is played from the shoulders up", according to Milfred "Deacon" Palmer. What did he know, you might ask? Enough to equip son, Arnold, with a mind and game that took the world of golf by storm in the late 1950s and 1960s.

But was he right? Over the years, top golfers are often asked the question, "what percentage of the game is technical and what mental?" And while not all would agree with Deacon Palmer, the majority would afford the mental side at least 50% status, and none would rate it low enough to dismiss as irrelevant.

Once most golfers have been playing for a certain length of time, the swing changes required to take them from where they are to where they'd like to be require more effort and practice than they're able or willing to give. Nick Faldo is probably the most notable exception, but how much time did he devote to it? Far more than you can probably spare! And what may feel like quite dramatic swing changes to us often barely register in the eyes of others.

So how can average golfers with swings that are far from technically perfect hope to improve significantly? While we'd stop short of saying that mental skills are easy to acquire or learn, we do believe that for most golfers they offer a more achievable road to improvement than a full swing makeover. In fact the potential for improvement due to mental skills is probably much higher proportionally for average golfers than for those who already swing the club well. Mental strength can overcome, or at least compensate for mechanical deficiencies. Yet all too often, the amount of time golfers devote to the technical side of the game is at best out of all proportion to, and at worst to the exclusion of, that which they devote to the mental side.

Some perhaps feel that if there's much they could be doing better technically, there's little point in pursuing new mental approaches. But this is simply not the case. Even if we can't swing perfectly, there's no logical reason why we should be able to produce a consistently repeatable swing for 15 holes, only for it to suddenly fall apart as we come down the stretch with victory, a personal best, or a much sought-after handicap cut at our mercy.

The stakes may not be as high for us in terms of reward or prestige as they are for top pros, but the feelings associated with either success or failure are often every bit as real. Winning a big club competition can bring delight equivalent to that of winning The Open; throwing away a golden opportunity can bring equal frustration and despondency.

There are many facets to mental fortitude on the course. For example, a greater degree of common sense could reduce our scores overnight without the need for any unusual mental skills. Most of us attempt at least one ridiculously foolish do-or-die shot a round – a brave recovery from the woods, or a shot over water that has a one-in-twenty chance of success. Yet invariably, though we've never practised these shots, our minds somehow convince us we can pull them off. Replacing just that one 'big number' with a percentage bogey could instantly knock two or three shots a round off our scores – and keep us in a good frame of mind rather than slipping into a card-wrecking red mist! Equally there are more specific mental skills that can enable us to cope better when we find ourselves facing a single crucial shot, or trying to get back to the clubhouse with a score intact as the internal pressure mounts. This book provides highly personalised accounts of both.

It adopts an informal, rather than academic style, offering privileged access to the minds of top British golfers in specific rounds, events or phases of their careers where the power of the mind helped them overcome internal and sometimes external adversity. There are also chapters with a top caddy and a top coach – the people at the coalface, if you like, of trying to guide their employers towards correct thinking both prior to and during tournaments. The narrative style throughout is deliberate. We think it makes for a better read than a series of specific mental skills lessons. So don't worry – we're not taking you back to school.

Many of the players' names you'll be familiar with, others perhaps less so. But all are gifted golfers for whom success more often than not depends on what goes on between the ears. Some of it may indeed just be common sense. But then, you can probably recall countless incidents on the course where in desperation, anger or panic, common sense went out of the window to your cost, provoking the kind of cold light of day 'if only I'd done that…' post-round analysis you hear in every golf club bar. Imagine how much more success you might enjoy if you were in mental control enough to do 'that' more often.

There are other mental skills that go beyond just common sense and will require some work on your part. You'll discover here examples of some of the skills various players have adopted to help them cope. You may simply be able to replicate what they have done, but equally you may need to seek expert advice. If you're serious about your game and want to improve you should be no less concerned about seeking the advice of a sports psychologist than you would in turning to a qualified PGA pro. In the same way that there is little point in going to an orthopaedic surgeon if you have a heart problem, there's little point getting your swing remodelled if your golfing problem lies in the mind.

Strangely, it is often the golfers who dismiss the concept of golf's mental side most vociferously who are the ones found uttering words like confidence and pressure most often. Your body and muscles feel neither confidence nor pressure – nor any other emotion you might experience on the course. They happen in your mind, which then processes them and passes them onto your body and muscles. If what is passed on is ineffective then your body will respond in an ineffective way; if it's effective then more effective physical performance can result.

This series of mini-biographies will allow you to see what went on under the mental bonnets of top players at key moments of rounds, tournaments or careers. We've applied no filter – you'll enjoy direct access to their minds via direct quotes. We've then sought to interpret – where necessary – in a way that can make their experiences meaningful, and hopefully beneficial, to you. Sometimes, if you so choose, you can go and play where they were playing, and stand where they were standing – on the 18th tee at Royal Porthcawl like Gary Wolstenholme in the 1995 Walker Cup, needing to win the hole despite giving yards away to Tiger Woods, or 200 yards out on the 17th fairway at the Forest of Arden like Greg Owen in the 2003 British Masters knowing one perfect shot would finally give him that elusive victory, or on the opening tee at Carnoustie just like 16-year-old Zane Scotland in 1999 facing his first shot in the Open Championship in front of hundreds of spectators.

This unique book's first-hand accounts and informal style seek to make it easy for you to read so you can then reap maximum benefit from it. Overall, it simply aims to make you rethink the way you think on the course.

Finally, take heart – the record books are as full of quirky swingers who have apparently over-achieved as they are of textbook swingers who barely made it past the first rung on the ladder to golfing superstardom. It's highly likely that more often than not this is at least partially down to the way both have chosen to think out on the course.

Faldo's major finale

Nick Faldo

When Nick Faldo entered the final round of the 1996 Masters lying second to Greg Norman, it had been nearly four years since he'd last tasted major success. And with Greg six shots clear, thanks in no small measure to a record-equalling opening 63, few gave Nick much chance when the pair teed off together on that final day. Yet four hours later he had emerged the victor by five, in one of the most astonishing major championship turnarounds ever. Here's how he thought his way through that dramatic Sunday.

"The key thing for me really was commitment to the decision. Once you've made the decision, 'right I'm going to do that' then you really commit to it and don't then change your mind halfway down or just before you go. You've decided to hit it there, so do it – and that's it. And if you then do it, you go 'great'. That's all you can do."

When Greg Norman fought through windy conditions to add a 3rd round 71 to opening efforts of 63 and 69 in the 1996 Masters, he had stretched his lead to a seemingly unassailable six shots and many felt the tournament was effectively over. His nearest challenger was five-times major winner and two-times Masters champion, Nick Faldo, but a 3rd round 73 appeared to have scuppered any hopes the Englishman had of notching up major number six.

Both men appeared to be saying the right things in the local Augusta press ahead of Sunday from their respective positions – certainly for anyone still hoping for any sort of a contest. "I've got a lot of work to do; I've got 18 tough holes," said Greg, while Nick asked: "Who knows what's in store tomorrow? If

I shoot a 65 or 66, it could get me in the right direction." But few others really felt that the final round would prove anything other than a formality, and come Sunday night Greg would finally be slipping on the Green Jacket that had eluded him throughout his career. There'd been a wildly blocked approach to the 18th in 1986 to give the title away, Larry Mize's outrageous play-off chip-in the following year to cruelly snatch it away from him, and a number of other heartbreaking near misses. The Masters owed Greg Norman, and Sunday April 14, 1996 was going to be pay back time.

At the time 41-year-old Greg was probably ahead of 38-year-old Nick at least on paper, with many feeling Nick's finest days were perhaps behind him. His last tour win had been at the Doral-Ryder Open over a year before, and although his early 1996 form in the States had been pretty good with three top 10s, his final pre-Masters outing at The Players Championship had yielded a missed cut. Greg was having a mixed year too, and after inheriting Nick's Doral-Ryder crown in March he'd then missed consecutive cuts at Bay Hill and The Players Championship ahead of the Masters.

But those missed cuts paled into insignificance when Greg started his Masters campaign with a scintillating 63 that left him, not surprisingly, leading and feeling good about his game. When he still led comfortably on Saturday evening, he was looking forward to Sunday with a sense of anticipation: "I've been there before and there is no better feeling than having a chance of winning a major championship. I'm going to enjoy the moment. I'm going to go to the 1st tee tomorrow as relaxed and comfortable as I have been since the first day."

Those who watched Greg that final day will question just how relaxed and comfortable he really was come the crunch, but even though a bogey on the 1st cut his lead to five straightaway, a birdie on the 2nd gave little indication of the horrors that lay ahead. Nick recalls those early holes: "I'd detected as early as the 2nd tee that he'd started regripping the club more than normal.

But then he made a great birdie there, showing great touch on the green, so I thought, 'he's okay, he's alright.' Then he mishit a shot up four, but although I saw shots happening I was really just doing my own thing."

That mishit on the 4th resulted in another dropped shot for Greg, but with Nick mixing a couple of early birdies with a bogey on the 5th, the lead was still four with 11 to play. Only then did things start to take a serious turn for the worse for Greg. A pulled second shot on the 8th left him scrambling for par while Nick made birdie, and when Greg spun his approach viciously off the front of the 9th green for his third bogey of the day, his lead was down to just two as the pair entered Augusta's famous back nine where the tournament is often said to really begin.

If the tournament does indeed begin there, then Greg got off to the worst possible start by bogeying 10 and 11 before hitting it into the water for the second consecutive day on 12 and running up a double bogey. With Nick parring those same holes, Greg's two-shot lead had become a two-shot deficit in less than an hour, and one from which he never really looked like recovering despite a brave birdie to match Nick's on 13 and an agonising lip-out for eagle on the 15th that saw Greg slump to his knees in anguish. That anguish was complete moments later on the par-3 16th when he hooked his 6-iron into the water for another double bogey, gifting Nick a four-shot cushion with just two to play and effectively sealing his fate.

When Nick birdied the 18th shortly afterwards to extend the final margin to five, the unimaginable turnaround was complete. Nick had shot a near-flawless 67; Greg an error-strewn 78 for an incredible 11-shot swing. Did Greg give it away or did Nick win it? Much post-event analysis has favoured the former argument, but this chapter looks at how Nick approached things from start to finish during that most memorable of Masters Sundays in the firm belief that a six-shot lead was not impregnable.

The initial goal

Although few pundits and golf fans were giving much credence to the prospect of Greg squandering a six-shot lead, Nick had been playing long enough to know that anything is possible in golf – perhaps more so at Augusta than anywhere because of the way water can play havoc with both mind and scorecard on those famous back nine par-3s and par-5s. So rather than resigning himself to playing for the runners-up spot, Nick had not given up on the title by any means, and had a very specific idea of where he needed to be heading into the crucial final nine: "My first goal was to get within three shots after nine holes – that was the first goal, because I thought three shots on the back nine at Augusta is nothing – the difference between a good hole and a bad hole; a birdie to a double; done! So that was the first game plan and then you just took it shot after shot." Normally such specific outcome-based goals would not be recommended. But in this instance, because Nick had set himself a target he knew to be a sensible possibility rather than an unrealistic pipedream, it was probably a good idea as it helped generate some hope in his mind for the round ahead.

So when he had surpassed that goal after nine holes through a combination of his good play and Greg's problems he knew for sure that victory was a possibility. Despite this, he refused to change tack to try and force things in response to what was happening around him, preferring to stick rigidly to his game plan and letting things take care of themselves.

The Master strategist

Many pros will tell you that Augusta is out on its own when it comes to strategic demands. The tee-shots may not always be the most visually intimidating – though recent changes to the layout have had some bearing on that – but you have to find the right part of the fairway to then give yourself a decent chance of finding the right part of the green, because it is in the approach play and on the greens that the course really bares it teeth. On many holes you simply have to be in the right place just to make par, and missing on the wrong side means you're dead. Just ask Justin Rose, whose miss to the left of the 17th on Masters Sunday in 2007 left him little chance of holding the green with his chip, let alone getting it close, thus effectively ending his spirited challenge.

Nick describes just how important it is to have a special strategy at the Masters compared to other events: "At Augusta you don't set the obvious goal. There's the pin, and people think you aim at the pin – but at Augusta you don't. First you have to make a decision about where you're going to miss it – short, right, left, long or whatever – and then you have to have the discipline to do it. You might be standing there with a wedge in your hand, thinking 'well I can hit this at the pin', but you know that if you hit it 10 feet behind the hole, you're stuffed. So you're far better off missing it 20 feet right. But that's almost against your instincts… you know, 'I've got a wedge in my hand, I'm not trying to hit it 20 feet right.'"

But such is the siren-like lure of the flagstick that many golfers find it hard to adopt such a disciplined approach. We quickly forget that it's far easier to two putt for par from 30 feet than it is to get up and down for bogey from the water in front of the green which has swallowed up our ill-advised attempt to attack a 'sucker pin' – as they're appropriately known. And it's harder still to force ourselves to stick to such a strategy for an entire round, resisting any temptation to deviate from it regardless because we know it represents our best chance of scoring. But as Nick goes on, that is exactly what you may have to do on certain courses: "At Augusta, you know that that is the place to go and you play to your safety nets all the time. It requires mental discipline to just stand there and say, 'I've got a game plan and I'm not going to change it. I'm not going to try and pull off the miraculous shot right now because that's not the percentage play. The percentage is to hit it there, 15 feet right of the pin'. And if you do it you say, 'great – that's just what I was trying to do.'"

Certain golf courses and holes place less rigorous demands on precise strategy than others, and the wisest golfers know the difference and are able to adapt their approach accordingly. At those where the penalty for missing in the wrong place is less severe, you can perhaps afford to adopt a slightly more aggressive game plan, as long as you're then disciplined enough to know when and where such a strategy can seriously backfire. But only you will know the courses and holes you play that need to be treated like Augusta based on the solid evidence you have accumulated from your past experiences of playing them.

Taking it shot by shot

As things continued to develop in Nick's favour that afternoon and he began to whittle away at Greg's lead, there must surely have come a time when he was tempted to start thinking, 'I've got him now; let's go in for the kill'. But the best players stick to their strategy and Nick is adamant that this was not the case. So while he was certainly taking note of everything going on around him, it didn't make the slightest bit of difference to the focused, shot-by-shot approach he'd chosen to adopt: "It was perhaps my best ever example of 'one shot at a time'. I just kept piecing it all together as things were really unfolding around me."

Many of us play in exactly the opposite way to this – often to our downfall. Yes, we sometimes set out with the noble intention of playing the course a certain way, vowing to hit certain clubs off certain tees. But as things evolve we're all too easily swayed from our game plans. Perhaps we bogey a hole we would normally regard as a birdie hole, or see our playing partner enjoy a two-shot swing when they birdie and we bogey. It's easy then to crack and reach for the driver on the next tee out of frustration or desperation, when it had been our pre-round intention to just hit a 4-iron for position. And it's at those times when we veer away from our game plans in a knee-jerk reaction to what's going on around us that we're at our most vulnerable out on the course. Most golfers will be able to relate to this all too readily!

Don't change a thing

Nick's approach that day was designed to guard against the dangers of a changeable strategy and he made it his overriding priority to stick to the plan regardless. He was able to carry it off to perfection when the temptation for less strong-minded individuals might have been to get caught up in all the excitement as Greg's lead began to evaporate, and lose sight of the original game plan.

As we've already seen, Nick had detected from quite an early stage that things weren't quite right with Greg, but this didn't trigger any thoughts about going for the jugular in response. Looking back on that day, Nick says: "No I didn't change anything. I felt the most important thing was not to change anything and to just keep on doing my own thing. I think that's the best message you can send out to your opponent... 'hey, I'm alright, I'm doing my own thing.'"

Not that Nick was trying to 'be' or 'do' anything. He was just going about his own business and taking care of the things that he could control. Whatever Greg did was beyond his control. That's all you should ever be looking to do on the golf course, because ultimately the only thing you really have almost total control over is what you do. It's possible that this may then have some bearing on what others do, but for the most mentally tough players the opposite should not hold true. What others do should have no bearing on what you do if you just stick to the process you've set yourself, except perhaps in matchplay, where it may sometimes be prudent to revise your strategy in response to the shot your opponent has just hit. Knowing when to play the course and when to play the opponent is a key skill to have. In that final round Nick was so immersed in doing the former that what Greg was doing was almost irrelevant to how he went about his business.

Just do your own thing

Perhaps there was no better example of this than on the par-5 13th where Nick produced what many have subsequently described as his masterstroke – a precision 2-iron to the heart of the green. Nick doesn't quite see it that way – though obviously delighted with the outcome – preferring to view it as just another 'one shot at a time' moment. He was playing first into this reachable par-5 guarded by Rae's Creek, and in range in two, but insists that the decision to go for it was not an attempt to send out a message to Greg, but rather one borne out of logical thought processes in keeping with his game plan. After Nick had found the green, Greg subsequently laid up, but Nick wasn't aware he was going to do so before playing his shot, and says it wouldn't have influenced his decision to go for it anyway as he was just focusing on doing his own thing.

Nick takes up the story: "The ball was more than slightly above my feet. It was well above my feet and on a downhill lie – so that tests your striking ability, that one! I don't 'try' to do something, as I say, but just by being yourself you are sending a great message, and I just wanted to hit the thing on the green because that's going to automatically send a message. I think that's the best thing. If the other player's unflappable, then what am I going to have to do to beat him because he's going to keep doing this? It's like playing against Borg, isn't it? He's not going to mishit a forehand so you try to get him on his backhand and that means that you're then adjusting to him. The whole goal that day was just to play my own game. On 13 there was some indecision with the second shot, but I wanted to go for it. I felt comfortable, I felt fine, but I just needed to find the right club and that was really it." Whatever your ability, there is a right shot and a right club for every situation, and it's when we try to break free from that and try something different that things so often go wrong. So before Nick pulled the trigger, he made sure he had the right club, he knew he had the ability, and he believed that although it was undoubtedly a tough shot, it was also the right shot to play.

Those who watched the TV coverage will know that Nick's 2-iron fizzed away arrow-straight towards the green setting up a relatively straightforward two-putt birdie. And although Greg got up and down to match him, it was another great example of Nick just focusing 100% on what he wanted to do and the processes involved in that, completely shutting out what Greg may or may not have been about to do in response. That was of no consequence to Nick as he weighed up that shot. He simply did what he wanted to do, letting everything else take care of itself rather than dictating what he did. And after that magnificent shot came off perfectly, surely there were feelings of euphoria and excitement? Not quite. Nick describes his reactions in this almost matter-of-fact way: "Well, yes, that's what I wanted to do and I did it, so sure you've got that buzz, that good feeling. But it's still one shot at a time. You've still got to get to the putt, you've got to work on that, and then you're off up 14 and so on. Sure it all helps, but you can't stay there."

That's something we've all probably been guilty of at some stage on the course – staying right there with all the emotions and excitement of one great shot, rather than quickly realising that there's still work to be done either on that hole or for the remainder of the round. One great shot may make a great talking point in the bar afterwards, but its significance will be somewhat diluted if you then got so carried away in the heat of the moment that the rest of the round became a complete write-off. Enjoy the great shots by all means, but just as it is unwise to dwell on the bad ones, don't linger too long to the detriment of what still has to be done.

It's never over till it's over

Many golfers, and other athletes, have celebrated prematurely either outwardly or inwardly, only to subsequently come unstuck through either getting ahead of themselves or perhaps switching off too soon. But Nick was well aware of the potential dangers here. It's easy to say with hindsight that Greg was a spent force by this stage because of everything that had happened to him. But actually he was still only two behind with five to play and the tournament was far from over. On the 15th, Greg's eagle chip lipped out agonisingly while Nick had to get up and down to match his birdie, and if those two things had both gone the other way in Greg's favour, the pair would have been tied with three to play and the momentum could so easily have shifted.

At no stage did Nick ever think it was over until he was safely on the final green in two with a four-shot lead. So when Greg dumped it in the water on 16 to generate that comfortable cushion, Nick knew that there was still work to do and refused to picture himself slipping on the Green Jacket just yet: "Even when Greg hit it in the water at 16 to give me a four-shot lead I thought, 'I just want to get to the 18th tee with four shots. I'm not going to give another one away.' So I hit a good tee shot down 17 and the same thing on 18 and I thought, 'if I hit the green in two here, then I can celebrate.' There was no counting any chickens until that last green, where I could just about kick it in the hole with a two-shot penalty and still survive!"

While it may be a little too fatalistic and negative to say 'expect the unexpected', it is certainly wise to at least realise that the unexpected can – and often does – happen, as golf's history books will only too willingly testify. And losing when you'd convinced yourself there was no way you could do so can be an awfully bitter pill to swallow and deal with in the weeks and months ahead.

In his time, Nick was widely considered to be as mentally strong as Tiger is now, so in addition to taking things one shot at a time and refusing to be swayed from his game plan he was also employing a range of other mental skills that he had learnt and refined over the years to help him cope on that final day…

… turn up the concentration

As events developed throughout the front nine and early part of the back nine it would have been easy for Nick to get caught up in the atmosphere and general buzz of the crowd as he ate into Greg's lead. But as we've said, although he was aware of what Greg was doing, he chose to concentrate purely on what he wanted to do and the processes involved in that, rather than what the potential result might be of everything that was going on around him.

Nick recounts that rather than getting distracted away from his game plan by the unfolding drama, he used it as the inspiration to focus even harder on what he was trying to do: "I noticed Greg's second shot on eight, and then the one on nine, but the one that was really an unforced error was on 10 where he pulled an 8-iron and then jammed his chip shot. I thought, 'wow, he's really feeling it now.' And that was really the time just to go even more inside yourself. It was just a little bit more than the normal effort. I had to just turn up the effort level to make the process happen – that's the best way of describing it. There was a discipline in the way you had to play each shot and I had to put just a bit more emphasis into how I did it."

... give yourself time

Another trick Nick had up his sleeve was the ability to control his breathing and keep things on an even keel when the tendency might be to start rushing your shots and the speed with which you move around the course as things start to happen. You may be able to remember times when you've had a good score going and have then found yourself walking faster between shots, ending up at your ball well ahead of your playing partners – speeding up at the very moment when it's probably wisest to slow things down.

Nick knew how important it was to guard against this and made sure that he had a coping strategy for situations like that: "You've got to be calm, you've got to be able to control your breathing and you've got to start slowing things down. I was self-taught on that, just to slow the breathing and everything down and just be yourself. You have to tell yourself sometimes to slow it down. Just slow down and give yourself that quiet moment and the time to do things – that's the important thing – so you can look at it and sense what you want to do and never feel rushed or anything."

... see it, feel it

Visualisation – the ability to mentally rehearse what you want to do before going ahead and doing it – can be a key skill in golf because the nature of the sport, unlike many others, allows you ample time to do it immediately before every shot. Of course, things can then intervene that mean the resulting shot doesn't quite come off as you'd pictured – if that were not the case, visualisers would hit perfect shots every time! But it's another useful weapon to have in your arsenal as you seek to take every step possible to enhance your chances of delivering on the course.

There are a couple of alternative visualisation methods available to you. You can either mentally picture yourself hitting the shot from the perspective of an external observer, or you can mentally rehearse it as it will appear through your own eyes. And there's no need to restrict yourself to just pictures either – with a little practice it's equally possible to imagine the feel and sounds associated with what you're trying to do too. Different players will find different methods more helpful.

Nick has used both techniques throughout his career, and called them into action that Masters Sunday to help him through: "There are two ways I do it. I can either stand back and actually see myself do it – I think at that time that's what I was really doing – or I can put the sensations inside myself, make my practice swing and see the ball fly exactly how I want it to fly. The pictures are usually pretty vivid – well they were at that time, I've probably got a bit vaguer now – but then it was usually pretty strong, and I'd make sure I had seen what I wanted to do before going ahead and doing it."

Many top players employ visualisation techniques, but it is something every golfer can incorporate into their games. It may be that you need to seek expert help in the initial stages to really learn this skill, but equally you may be able to work things out for yourself. Why not try storing away in your mind specific occasions when you have executed shots perfectly with each club in the bag, then try and recall as vivid an image in your mind as possible of how that looked and felt next time you face a similar shot with each relevant club. Or perhaps visualise yourself producing good shots in pressure situations like the dreaded 1st tee shot or coming down the stretch with a handicap cut on the line.

... make your experience count

The age-old adage that experience counts is undeniably true, but only of maximum consequence if it is direct experience and backed up by ability. You can have all the general experience in the world, but if what you're attempting this time is beyond your ability it may not yield the results you crave. It's that 'learning how to win' thing that commentators often refer to. But when direct experience and ability come together they form a powerful alliance that can make all the difference.

Nick knew on that Masters Sunday that he not only had the ability to win, but also the experience of winning on that very same stage twice before. He felt that this helped in two ways – firstly because there was no danger of him being overawed by the occasion and secondly because it allowed him to devise a specific game plan that he knew from experience would directly answer the questions the course would be asking: "Sure you can keep saying to yourself, 'hey I've been here before, I'm comfortable with all this.' But you also know what you're doing, and you automatically know your game plan which is great. For example, you know where the pin is going to be on 16, so you've already made a decision about where you're going to hit the ball there."

In both instances, direct experience helps by eliminating doubt – firstly because Nick knew from similar past experiences that he was more than capable of standing up to the pressures of the occasion, and secondly because he knew that come Sunday there would be no tricky decisions to make about which parts of the greens to play for on many holes.

Those who watched that final round will recall that while Greg appeared ill-at-ease, fidgety and uncomfortable, Nick appeared cool, calm and collected. Greg had won countless tournaments worldwide including majors, but the Masters was the one he really wanted, and he had no direct experience of winning that specific event – in fact only a number of unfortunate memories. Nick, on the other hand, had been there and succeeded twice before so knew exactly what would be required.

... stay in the present

Perhaps the strongest message of all to come out of this chapter with Nick is the absolute necessity of staying firmly in the present on the golf course. It's easy to get a little bit cynical about the clichéd way in which this phrase is trotted out. But clichés are often only clichés because they're so true that there really isn't any other way of expressing them. That's certainly the case with this one.

Nick is certain that staying in the present moment was one of the key contributing factors to his success that day, when amid the unfolding events, he could so easily have allowed himself to be pulled this way and that mentally: "All the way round it was just a case of 'stay right here – right, what do you want to do on this shot? You can't look ahead to another hole.' And I think it was one of my best ever examples of being only in the present time."

It's been said many times before and will be said many times again in this book and elsewhere – on the golf course, you can't undo what's been done, and you can't influence what might happen several holes ahead by thinking about it before you actually get there. The only thing you have direct influence over is the next shot you face, and that shot alone should therefore occupy all your thought processes. So try and banish 'if only' and 'what if?' from your mind's on-course vocabulary and replace them simply with 'right, what does this next shot require?'

It may be that you need to develop a specific trigger to help you do this – perhaps a key word or physical action – so that when you do find your mind wandering back to shots you let slip on previous holes or ahead to the tough shots yet to come, you have a strategy in place to bring you instantly back to the all-important present. That trigger might be a suitably descriptive word such as 'calm' or 'anchor' or it could involve bringing to mind the name or on-course demeanour of a renowned cool, calm customer like Faldo or Langer perhaps.

Self-belief

To conclude this chapter with Nick we felt it would have been remiss not to ask Britain's most prolific major winner of the modern era exactly what it feels like when you're out there in contention on the final day with one of golf's biggest prizes on the line. Does it ever become the walk in the park that a calm exterior sometimes hints at, especially when you've got the experience that Nick has? Far from it, as Nick explains: "You have to have self-belief so that you're out there and you enjoy it – that stomach-churning – you're out there thinking, 'this is great; this is what I've practised for.' You've got to be comfortable standing there; you're nervous – just short of shaking because you are in control – but it's a hell of a feeling going through you. The adrenaline is unbelievable, because you're running purely on intensity – that's the other word I'd use – because you've got to get the right intensity. How do you rev your engine? That, I thought, was a key thing – getting the right intensity throughout the day."

In terms of self-belief, Nick was right up there with Tiger and Jack in his heyday. And it is self-belief that enables great players to welcome, rather than fear that stomach-churning experience, because they know it's an inevitable part of the process if they're to succeed at the very highest level. This has been described by some as 'fire in the belly but ice in the head' and it's ultimately all about how you interpret those feelings. The very best players see them as perfectly normal and, perhaps more importantly, manageable.

It's unlikely you'll ever get to play at a similar level to Nick unless you're extremely talented. But whatever level you do play at, getting into contention in an event regarded as one of the big ones – your club championship perhaps – can trigger the same emotions, fears and anxieties. And it is then that self-belief can come to your rescue. But is it something you either have or don't have, or something only the very best can really aspire to? No – any golfer can have self-belief to match their technical ability, such that they know they're capable of producing the golf they need to produce to play at the level they're trying to play at – whatever level that is.

But exactly what is self-belief beyond just a glib phrase trotted out by countless athletes who are aware it's a positive thing to say, but perhaps less sure what really underlies it? Self-belief is more about knowing you're doing the right things than just doing things right. It means developing a balanced perspective on your strengths and weaknesses and an awareness that you need to tackle the latter if you're to improve; it means you're sometimes prepared to take risks and make decisions without fear of being wrong, even if things don't always turn out perfectly; it means you can recover from setbacks with a renewed sense of focus and energy rather than giving up; it means confining self-criticism to your practice sessions and steering clear of it on the course where it can wear you down mentally; it means setting and striving to achieve process-driven goals that will actually stretch you, rather than purely result-driven ones, and it means developing robust ways of dealing with pressure, as ably demonstrated by Nick throughout this chapter.

The important thing is that self-belief goes far deeper than mere form or results. It can be a driving force that allows you to achieve way more than what others are perhaps expecting based on the outward evidence that they can see. When Nick teed it up in that 1996 Masters he hadn't finished in the top 10 there for five years, the top 20 for three years, or won anywhere in the world for 13 months. Yet when he got himself in the hunt he had something far more deep-rooted than mere results to call on that allowed his mind to override all that. We'll leave the final word to Nick: "The reason I think that round was so special was that I wasn't as confident going into that Major as [I was for my previous major win] in 1992. So I really had to go through the process. I would have genuine doubts and I'd be thinking, 'can I keep this going?' or whatever. And so it was probably my best ever example of talking to someone as it were – 'what do you want to do and how are you going to do it?' – and then visualising the shot. I think the secret is that you just do what you feel comfortable with and don't compromise yourself in any way."

Rise, fall and rise

Justin Rose

Few golfers have burst onto the professional scene quite as dramatically as Justin Rose. But after the incredible high of finishing 4th in the 1998 Open at Royal Birkdale as an amateur, his first professional start the following week kicked off a run of 21 consecutive missed cuts. How did he cope with the pressures and disappointments of that period at just 18 years of age, and was it, with hindsight, a blessing in disguise?

"At the time it was just heartbreak after heartbreak. But I never really lost sight of the light at the end of the tunnel – I always felt I was going to pull through and I was going to get there. There were times when I didn't know when, or how long I was going to have to keep grinding it out. But the thing that kept me going was the deep-seated belief that 'I am good enough. I've just got to pull through this.'"

In July 1998 a 17-year-old Englishman turned pro. Nothing exceptional in that – plenty of youngsters do so in their late teens to embark on their PGA training. But quite exceptional in that this particular youngster, Justin Rose, had just holed a miracle pitch shot to birdie the 72nd hole and finish 4th in The Open at Birkdale as an amateur, and that his first job as a trainee professional would be to tee it up in the following week's Dutch Open rather than changing the captain's spikes in the workshop.

Sadly, there the fairytale ended – at least temporarily. For what happened next was one of professional golf's most celebrated runs of missed cuts ever – 21 in total – all played out in the full glare of constant national press publicity. As

Justin recalls: "There was front page and back page stuff for a good few weeks. And I was never really prepared for that sort of introduction to pro golf." Circumstances dictated that he had no chance of slipping quietly into his chosen profession as many other youngsters are able to, because his sensational exploits at The Open had made him the next British superstar-in-waiting and everyone was watching his every move very closely.

Some were sympathetic to his plight, others adopted a 'told you he was too young' attitude and many surmised that the decision to turn pro was nothing but a hasty response to his success in The Open. Justin points out that was not the case: "The decision was made when I failed to win the British Amateur Championship in the June before The Open. The Dutch Open and Scandinavian Masters had kindly already given me invites to play in them as a pro even before The Open had taken place." The plan was that the decision to turn pro would only subsequently have been delayed had Justin won the Amateur Championship and therefore earned the right to compete in the following year's Masters at Augusta.

Starting with that Dutch Open, his first few professional tournaments were a series of near misses, with Justin falling the wrong side of the cut by one or two shots. But as the pressure to perform mounted, so unfortunately did his scores, and the margins became progressively wider as he continued to miss out on weekend action in every tournament he played for the remainder of 1998. The winter break brought no change of fortune and it was more of the same for the first six months of 1999 until finally, at the Compaq Grand Prix of Europe at Slaley Hall, a second round 69 cleared him for weekend duty for the first time in 11 months, and for the first time as a professional.

The third round 82 that he then went on to shoot there on the Saturday probably didn't really matter. The deadlock had been broken and from then on the progress would be slow but sure. The following year he came within a hair's breadth of retaining his tour card. He got it back comfortably at the annual tour qualifying school before kicking off the 2001 season with two 2nd place finishes on the European Tour's South African leg. He ended up 33rd on the Order of Merit that year and 9th the following year after his breakthrough tour win in the Dunhill championship and subsequent first victory on home soil in the British Masters. Then, after another solid year in 2003 with six top 10s in the first half of the season, Justin decided it was time to spread his wings and make America's PGA Tour his main base from 2004 onwards.

He had successfully come through the dark times to establish himself as a top-class player. This chapter takes a closer look at how he coped with that 11-month spell when he didn't earn a penny as a professional, and whether or not it equipped him better for his golfing future.

Mounting pressure from within and without

Part of Justin's problem was that his unique circumstances affected how he saw his early days as a professional. The remainder of 1998 was originally supposed to have been a good learning experience ahead of November's tour qualifying school, but he began to see the extra opportunities his Open heroics afforded him as a chance to actually bypass it. Rather than just turning up and playing golf, there was a calculator constantly on the go in his mind as to how much he needed to earn to secure his card. But he was only 17 – 18 the second week on tour – and these thoughts took him ahead of himself, prompting unrealistic expectations and generating unnecessary pressure from within. As Justin explains: "I began to believe not that it would be a bonus to get my card, but to expect to get my card from the seven events that I played. Every week I would turn up thinking 'okay, if I finish 2nd or 3rd this week I'll have my card.' But I think at the age of 17 – and hindsight's a wonderful thing – the important thing is that you're just improving as a player. So I think what happened at Birkdale changed my expectations and I ultimately put a lot of pressure on myself."

As the bad run continued, Justin began to tinker and change things that didn't really need changing: "I began to maybe work harder in an effort to get better and maybe just stretched myself out a little bit. All of a sudden, from playing well, you're just questioning your form. I never really questioned my deep-down talent or ability, but at the time you question your form." Form that had been good enough for 4th place in The Open just weeks earlier – something that many very good players don't come close to achieving throughout their entire careers.

Justin has since gone on to say that whereas he'd been able to approach that 1998 Open with "raw amateur enthusiasm", in those early days as a professional he allowed himself to be sucked into changing the processes that had served him so well at Royal Birkdale.

There were pressures from without too that weighed heavily on Justin's young shoulders. The press were naturally taking a keen interest in his early professional career and he found it hard to shut out all the hype: "Obviously it shouldn't be added pressure, and now I'm much better-equipped to handle that sort of thing. But at the time your mind begins to race."

There were all sorts of other complicated things going on too that were distracting Justin from his primary job of simply playing golf. Achievements such as Justin's in The Open equate to potentially big endorsement money, and there was plenty of talk about how big a deal had been, or was about to be struck on his behalf. Justin recalls: "I didn't sign [a deal] the week after The Open which maybe some people think I did. But I did feel like every time I played I was influencing or affecting my value. And that was a lot of pressure to play under. I almost wished I'd had some sort of done deal. I felt that that was quite a big distraction and burden to carry." In this kind of situation, you can end up developing an image of yourself based on the way you perceive others to be seeing you. Trying to then live up to this perceived image becomes another burden on top of everything else, and golf can then begin to feel like another monkey on your back rather than a relief from the grind of other things going on in your life.

Many club golfers will testify that when there's important stuff going on in their lives, their golf sometimes tends to suffer. So it's probably no surprise that when Justin's game developed negative momentum amidst all this pressure, he found it very difficult to break the cycle.

Momentum – it cuts both ways

Golfers know that momentum can carry them a long way both ways, and that it's easy to feel powerless to resist it. It's more about confidence really – or lack of it – than fatalism, although many a golfer will at some stage have asked 'why me?' as disaster seems to follow disaster on the course.

For Justin, it could all have been so different if a couple of those early tournaments had just gone the other way for him. Amid all the '21 missed cuts' hype, very few people actually remember that Justin's second round as a professional was a 65 in the Dutch Open. Justin hasn't forgotten: "It's a momentum thing, golf. You get some momentum on your side and who knows what can happen. And certainly that 65 in the 2nd round was a hugely gutsy performance. I birdied the last hole to get back to level for the tournament and everyone was saying that level was going to be the cut. But the story goes – and I don't know if it's true – that some guy in the last group birdied the last to move the cut from level to one-under."

Hardly a disaster and still every reason to believe he could quickly build on his Open momentum. But next week a three-putt on the last saw him again miss out by a shot, and suddenly he began to change his attitude and goals for each tournament. Justin remembers: "I began to turn up at the golf course thinking 'hey, let's make the cut this week,' rather than going there with the attitude of 'I'm playing well, let's just focus shot by shot, see what happens and hopefully have a great week.'" The latter is a far better option as it isn't weighed down by clear-cut outcome goals. A missed cut with the former approach would constitute failure, whereas the same result from the latter perspective could still be viewed as a success if he'd adhered to his 'shot by shot' goal but things just hadn't worked out or the putts had refused to drop. The more specific you make your outcome goals, the more likelihood there is of failure – and failure does no-one's confidence any good.

Fortunately, momentum can work both ways. Just as it sometimes seems impossible to break a run of negative results, so too it can be relatively easy to feed off positive results. Justin remembers when things began to turn round for him: "I think it was in the European Open at the K Club in 2000. I holed something like a 40-footer on the 17th green and then a 45-footer on the 18th to make the cut and it was nice to finally feel like I'd pulled something out of the bag, rather than letting something slip. And that turned things round a little bit."

No 'one-trick pony'

Finishing 4th in The Open may have been a phenomenal achievement for a 17-year-old amateur, but there came a point where Justin felt it actually became a distorting factor as he tried to constantly live up to that one specific moment rather than everything that had gone before.

And when you examine everything that had gone before, it was already remarkable stuff but perhaps not quite in the same explosive league as that 4th place. Eventually, as he sought to find the deep-rooted confidence needed to carry him through that run of poor form, Justin was able to see that his amateur career was a better hook on which to hang his self-belief than one spectacular moment: "I tried to forget about the 4th place and look back on what I'd achieved in my amateur career. As an amateur I was definitely ahead of my time. I won the Carris Trophy at 14 and the McGregor Trophy at 14, which are the England U-18 and U-16 Championships. I'd got to the final stage of The Open qualifying at 14 and I was well on my way to believing 'I am going to be a great player.' So I tried to draw strength from that really and take The Open out of the equation – and that helped a lot."

It was only when the mists generated by his Open exploits began to clear away a little that he was able once again to see clearly everything that he'd achieved prior to it – and which had of course helped make it all possible. In that sense, Birkdale wasn't a one-off, but rather the culmination of an already successful amateur career. And when that earlier groundwork became the basis for his professional career again rather than one extraordinary achievement, the foundations for the future became more solid.

For you too, the mental foundations for your golf shouldn't be grounded in one particular round or moment. Those can certainly be inspirational, but they can also be misleading. Self-belief and confidence should really be built on a series of solid performances and achievements, or the setting of realistic process goals for your standard of play or the aspects of your game or technique you're most eager to develop.

Built to withstand pressure

Most competitors view the annual European Tour qualifying school as a six-round living nightmare unlike anything they've experienced before. As a result many fail to live up to their expectations or ability. But because of what Justin had been through, he saw it quite differently: "The way I perceived it, compared to how a lot of my friends and people I know well perceived it, I actually seemed to quite enjoy Q-school. All the experiences I'd had previously really helped me deal with pressure situations like that. So those are the kind of positives I can take out of that whole period now. I think I've become a lot stronger and more resilient all in all." His year of disappointment and intense media scrutiny had effectively fulfilled an adversity-conditioning role. It had toughened him up.

Short term adversity proved beneficial in the long run, and continued to do so early the following season after he had comfortably come through qualifying school. He finished 2nd in consecutive weeks in South Africa at the start of 2001, and although he didn't win, he was happy that when the opportunity arose, he didn't wilt under pressure. Justin explains: "That was when I first began to feel comfortable on tour. I had game – I always knew that. But it was nice to finally prove it. And I think the big thing was that I didn't crumble under pressure in both those tournaments. In fact I hardly put a foot wrong down the stretch. Adam Scott made a birdie on the last to beat me in one, and then Mark McNulty knocked in a 20-footer to beat me. That was a good confidence boost for me – the fact that I stood up and really proved myself to myself under pressure in the pro game."

Experience counts – even at 27

Even if the hardship of that year has ultimately given Justin a tougher edge, he would still rather not have gone through it. But he does feel that the long-term benefits are real: "I'd rather have had the seamless route into professional golf that Sergio Garcia had. But I think that when I'm in the middle of my career and bidding for majors consistently and things like that, the toughness that I gained from that period will hopefully see me through – that's what I like to believe anyway."

He also feels that if he ever suffered a sustained period of poor form again he would do very little different in response, choosing to focus on deep-rooted self-belief, and trusting that plenty of hard work would turn things round: "I believe the talent is there so it's just a matter of doing the day-to-day things to back it up. I'm a lot more mature about my game now in that I know why I play well or why I don't play well. I know what suits me and what doesn't suit me. There's a lot of learning under the belt that will stand me in good stead over the next few years. I feel one of my biggest attributes is experience which is a weird thing to say at such a young age. But that's what I think." Justin has come to know his game, and is well aware that talent is only half the story and can be seriously undermined if it's not backed up by hard work.

Ultimately, experience is experience, regardless of age. And even though there is obviously some correlation between the two, it's the type of experience that really counts. Someone who has had a trouble-free transition into the pro ranks may simply not know what to do when poor form sets in. Justin on the other hand, even though he is still only 27, has been there, knows all about it and feels confident that he will know how to respond should he ever again suffer to that degree. Really telling experiences are more about quality than quantity.

Hearing is not necessarily believing

There are always plenty of people to tell professional sportsmen how good they are – coaches, commentators, agents, fans – regardless of whether or not it's true. Being reminded of how good you are can, of course, be a big confidence booster – but it's only really of any use if it's actually true. If it's not true, then no amount of positive affirmation will be able to gloss over your shortcomings. Justin has a good attitude to all this: "I don't tend to believe people or trust people when they tell you how good you are. I'm very much a person who needs to see evidence for myself. It needs to come from within for me to totally believe it, trust it and draw strength from it." The opinions of others are not the greatest confidence builders.

Well-meaning people may try to motivate you by telling you how good you are based on your results or a few good shots that they happen to have seen you play. But only you will really know whether you've scraped it round and got away with it, or whether it was a solid performance suggesting real improvement. Don't believe what others say if you know in your heart it's not true. Ideally you need to be able to recognise your strengths and weaknesses yourself, regarding the latter as merely temporary and in need of some attention. Then, rather than simply practising what you're already good at, focus on resolving those weaknesses where the scope for improvement is the greatest. Like Justin, if you know your game well enough, you'll know what the truth is – and there's no point kidding yourself.

If you really want it, work hard!

Thankfully, Justin has come through his highly publicised slump to emerge as one of Britain's best young prospects. He has established himself as a very consistent performer in America, come perilously close to securing his maiden PGA Tour victory on a number of occasions, and become one of the 10 best players on the planet according to the Official World Golf Ranking thanks to a 2007 season in which he amazingly won the European Tour Order of Merit despite only playing in 12 qualifying events. Two wins, three runners-up spots and only one finish outside the top 12 sealed that particular deal. Perhaps even more significantly, he has proved he has the game to compete in golf's very biggest events, achieving top five finishes in the US Open, the WGC Matchplay and, most memorably, the 2007 Masters where he reached the 71st tee just one off the lead before an unfortunate double bogey put paid to his title chances.

Looking back to his earlier amateur career, there was every indication that this would be the case, but prolonged slumps have finished off the careers of many other young golfers before they've even really started.

Justin came through his lean spell on two main counts, neither of which are specifically about technique – firstly, he believed deep-down that he was good enough to make it and secondly, he knew that if he really wanted it he would have to knuckle down and work hard.

If you experience a loss of form, Justin's final words are worth dwelling on as you try to find your way out of it: "There's no substitute for hard work and determination. How much you really want it dictates how many knocks you can take. That's the question you've got to ask yourself: 'Is the hard work I have to put in really worth it? Do I really want it that much?' And if the answer's 'yes, I really want it,' then you've just got to do whatever you've got to do to pull through. There's no textbook way to regain your form, but you'll find a way if you really want to."

Scotland the brave

Zane Scotland

In the summer of 1999, top junior amateur, Zane Scotland, wasn't yet old enough to drive a car. But thanks to a remarkable series of performances, he did qualify to drive it off the 1st tee in the 128th Open Championship at Carnoustie along with the greatest names in professional golf. A tall enough order for anyone, let alone a mere 16-year-old schoolboy.

"I wasn't overwhelmed because I'd pictured in my head so many times what it would be like. So when I did actually get there I wasn't completely taken aback because it all seemed very real. I thought, 'you're supposed to be completely overawed by all this,' but it was almost as if I'd been there before."

The average teenage boy's thought processes are more likely to revolve around which girls to ask out, or which CDs to pump out than how to cope with playing alongside golf's superstars. But that's exactly what 16-year-old Surrey schoolboy, Zane Scotland, faced in July 1999 when he successfully battled through all the qualifying rounds to earn a spot at Carnoustie along with Tiger and all for one of the toughest Open Championships in living memory. That incredible achievement made him the youngest ever qualifier for the Open, though not its youngest ever competitor – a record that Young Tom Morris still holds 142 years after teeing up in the 1865 event at the tender age of just 14 years, 5 months and 25 days.

Playing carefree golf with your mates one minute and teeing it up with the greatest names in world golf the next seems an improbably wide gap to bridge. So how exactly did Zane Scotland, the boy, cope with being thrust headfirst into a man's world?

Boy he may have been, but in 1999 he already had a golf game that most adults would die for – a star player for club and county, part of the English Golf Union's School of Excellence, and the lowest-handicapped 15-year-old in the country the year before. To a certain extent, it was perhaps wide-eyed adolescence that allowed him to play down in his mind the magnitude of 1999's events, but Zane also used key mental skills to cope with their nerve-wracking demands.

Of course, rounds of 82 and 81 meant that he didn't come close to winning The Open. Nor did he make the cut by some considerable margin (though he did beat a shell-shocked Sergio Garcia by 9 shots!). But his achievement was really just getting to Carnoustie in the first place.

So just how did he do it? Well, assuming your handicap is sufficiently low, there are two stages to Open qualifying. First an 18-hole regional event attended by club professionals, their assistants and very low handicap amateurs, then a 36-hole final qualifier just prior to the main event at courses local to the Championship venue. Here, regional qualifiers are joined by non-exempt tour pros to compete for a handful of spots in what often become low-scoring shoot-outs – the notorious links weather permitting.

At the regional stage, a birdie on the final hole squeezed Zane into a play-off, which he duly won to give himself the slightly dubious honour of becoming 35th reserve for final qualifying. The chances of getting in from such a lowly position appeared so remote that Zane wouldn't even have bothered to make the speculative 500-mile trek north but for a friend who'd also qualified – and his dad's powers of persuasion. But he did. And then as he played the 15th hole at Downfield – one of the final qualifying venues – the day before the event started, a call came through on his mobile from the R&A – he was in! Not only that, but at Downfield, the very course on which he had by chance chosen to practise.

So next day Zane found himself teeing up alongside four-time European tour winner, Robert Allenby, and two days later, having shot a six-under par two-round total, he had defied all the odds to earn one of the coveted spots in the Open Championship itself, being played at Carnoustie for the first time in 24 years. Make no mistake – nerves were running rampant throughout this entire experience and in the Championship itself, but Zane was equipped with various nerve-management strategies that enabled him to perform on a stage that perhaps should have taken him way out of his depth.

So let's dip into Zane's memories of those two life-changing weeks to pinpoint some key moments and the mental skills he used to guide him through uncharted waters.

Seen it all before!

Those maintaining a sceptical approach to the power of visualisation may wish to reconsider after reading these two recollections of Zane's, one of which simply exploited the power of youthful imagination. In answer to his dad's question as to how he had coped on Carnoustie's practice ground among the Greg Normans and Darren Clarkes, Zane recounts: "I didn't even know they were there because I'd pictured so many times previously what it would be like to be on tour or to play in a major championship. So when I did get there, I wasn't completely taken aback. Daydreaming, as I had done, really set me up for it."

Picturing yourself in situations you've not yet experienced can make the reality far less alien than it otherwise might be. If you try and imagine the pressure you'll be feeling, the crowd noise all around you or actually standing on that 1st tee looking down the fairway at the shot you'll be facing, the mind doesn't always know how to differentiate between that and the actual event, which is what makes imagery such a powerful form of mental conditioning.

And if you thought your 1st tee nerves were bad, imagine being a 16-year-old on that 1st tee at Carnoustie facing some of the most brutal Open conditions of the modern era. Zane's initial concerns were simply whether he would even be able to walk over and tee it up without mishap. But when it came to the shot itself he remembers: "I was so nervous... I'd already thought 'I don't want to sky it or top it.' Then as I got over the ball I just thought to myself, 'imagine you're on the practice ground,' because I was really ripping my driver there. All these bad thoughts had been going through my head, but I looked up and just pictured the 250-yard board on the practice ground. And the ball came right out of the middle and went way out there."

Zane banished negative thoughts with images of previous relevant successes, enabling him to ultimately address that opening tee-shot with enhanced confidence.

Familiarity breeds... comfort

Surrounding yourself with what you know and are comfortable with is less likely to trigger a panic response than undertaking wholesale change when breaking new ground. Zane immersed himself in what he knew – his coach, his parents, his usual golf game – so he was better able to cope with the pressures of that week both on and off the course. Zane remembers: "The whole week, I tried to do things that I always do... even when I talked to the press I just tried to talk how I would normally talk if I was with friends. On the course I was trying to play like I would if I was with friends. I was always trying to do things that I knew."

Change can exaggerate any 'out of your depth' feelings, while keeping things as normal as possible can provide a cushion between you and the pressures of the new experience you're facing. The more you can make an important competition feel like a knockabout at your home club, the more comfortable you'll be out on the course. After all, in both scenarios if you break it down to basics, it's still you, a few clubs and a little white ball. Psychologists like to talk about something called the 'Ideal Performance State' or IPS. It's a changeable state, but the principle is that if you keep a diary of what sort of mood or state you're in when you perform best, you can then begin to get a handle on the key factors that lead to your personal IPS and the type of things that can help maintain it. Once armed with this information you can then try and pinpoint certain triggers that actually help you shift your mood from a poor state into one in which you're more likely to perform well. You don't necessarily have to be in your IPS to succeed as it's always possible to 'win ugly', but not only can it increase your chances of playing well, you'll also tend to enjoy it more because it feels so much better, and that can lead to an upward spiral in your golfing fortunes too. A kind of knock-on bonus effect.

And when circumstances fall your way, make the most of it. Zane was drawn with tour pro, Warren Bennett, at Carnoustie. Zane's father knew Warren's manager and had been trying to fix up a game for his son. So when Zane read the draw, that loose connection had a comforting effect. He had no control over it, but once it had happened he drew the maximum mental benefit from it.

Settle down now

Nerves can affect performance to a debilitating degree, so when the pressure's on it's good to find a settling influence. Zane enjoyed a number of these that week. In the first round at Downfield, having laid up on the par-5 3rd hole, he then semi-shanked his approach – a potential mental disaster in waiting. But he recalls: "I was so nervous. I'd just played a terrible shot but I laughed at myself and thought, 'you've just got to enjoy it.' I walked up and remember imagining I was still playing on the practice ground with my buddies. I played a great lob shot over the bunker and made par off a shank, and after that I thought 'if I can make par off a shank then I'll be okay.' I then hit a great tee shot, birdied the next hole, and all of a sudden just started to relax."

That round ended up as a four-under par 69 to get him right into contention, so it was no surprise that on the 1st tee the following day he was "obscenely nervous". But after an indifferent drive he played a decent approach and then sank a 20-footer for birdie to instantly settle the nerves. You can play good golf with nerves present – it's all about how you interpret those nerves and channel the feelings they generate. When it came to Carnoustie itself, Zane struggled through the front nine unaware of how much others were struggling too. He remembers: "I got to seven-over and I just really didn't want to embarrass myself. One of my mates in the crowd had heard that Garcia had started really badly, and I said 'what did Garcia shoot?' And he said '89.' That was such a big relief. I just thought, 'well I'm not going to shoot 89 whatever happens.' That was really good for me, and I made a couple of birdies on the back nine."

Critical moments

Reaching certain critical moments can also have a very positive influence on performance and Zane can specifically identify two such moments that freed him up to perform that week. The first was a dramatic change in his ball-striking after that phone call to say he'd got into final qualifying. Zane remembers: "I wasn't hitting the ball very well, then I got the phone call and all of a sudden for the last four holes I just ripped it because I was so excited." An end to all the waiting and uncertainty had triggered a tension release that allowed Zane to suddenly up his performance level. Then towards the end of the second round at Downfield, Zane holed a bunker shot on the 15th to snatch birdie from the jaws of bogey and reach the magical six-under par figure that he had in his mind as the qualifying mark: "I remember over those last few holes that because I'd reached the goal I'd set out to achieve, I was then really nervous – but confidently nervous. I had that little peace of mind from getting to the point where I wanted to be. I'd struggled for most of the round but when I got to that point, I started striking the ball much better and with more authority."

As it transpired, six-under qualified comfortably.

There must be a way

Zane was also shrewd enough to know there's more than one way to score, and when the perfect ball-striking avenue is temporarily sealed off for whatever reason, you simply have to find another way. In the regional qualifier Zane recalls: "I really wasn't hitting the ball very well, but my chipping and putting were just so good." He was confident in his ability to perform even on poor ball-striking days, and the magnitude of the occasion wasn't going to shake him from this positive approach: "I said, 'well you're up to it, play three decent [qualifying] rounds' – which I could do on any day in any given week – and that would be good enough. And that's what happened, I didn't have the mentality of having to play perfect golf, I just had the mentality of playing golf like I normally do. I wouldn't worry about how I was hitting the ball, because even when I was 16 I knew I could shoot five-, six- or seven-under par, even if I was hitting the ball terribly. Somehow I would find a way of doing it." Perfection may be unachievable, but managing imperfection effectively most certainly is not. Too often we get hung up about the need to play great golf in big tournaments or pressure situations to succeed. We then start doing things we wouldn't normally do or making rash decisions in response, when in reality good enough, safe golf is usually more than adequate.

Even when paired with proven European Tour winner, Robert Allenby, in final qualifying, Zane found ways to boost his confidence. How? He acknowledged that Allenby may have had the edge in many areas, but in others he could more than compete: "I thought to myself 'well he drives it so well,' but on the greens I noticed he didn't look that good. And I thought 'maybe I can't compete with him in terms of ball-striking, but I'm putting well and I can whip him on the greens.' And every putt I looked at just went in."

Good players can almost always find ways of competing and it's often said that the key to success in golf isn't how good the good rounds are so much as how good the bad rounds are. It is that ability to turn a potential 77 into a 72 on a bad day that separates the good from the very good player. In that respect there's no finer example than Tiger Woods who compensates for temporary deficiencies like no other golfer. When his driving is wayward he simply finds other ways of getting the ball in the hole in the desired number of strokes, and he has spoken many times about winning with different parts of his game when his ball-striking is off.

Watch and learn

Watching what's going on around you can help your game no end – and it's not just the good things you see, but also the bad that can have a positive impact. In the final qualifier Zane remembers Robert Allenby getting quite wound up, even accusing Zane of slow play and walking on his throughline beyond a putt. Zane used this to his advantage: "I thought, if you're worried about the throughline, then you're not thinking about making the putt!"

When Zane saw that Allenby was getting ever more ruffled and agitated as events seemed to be conspiring against him, he used that to his advantage too, even though he was at the kind of age far more likely to be committing those particular crimes himself. Zane remembers: "The more wound up he got, the more that relaxed me, because I could see how silly it looked and even at 16 I could see how detrimental it was. It's much easier to see it when someone else is doing it, and I thought 'it's really not helping him' and I relaxed even more I suppose. I learned really quickly from what he was doing. I thought, 'well if he's getting wound up and he's not playing very well then I don't want to get wound up because it's not helping.'" The upshot? Zane ended up in the starting line-up at Carnoustie. Learning to control your emotions can give you a big edge over someone who has lost control of theirs.

Take it away with you

So those are some of the key thought processes that helped Zane through his nerve-wracking Open ordeal. The crucial thing is being able to then take those experiences away with you and use them to your advantage another day. Taking yourself out of your comfort zone and coming through mentally unscathed can have a meteoric effect on confidence levels back in a lesser environment. If you want to try building up your confidence why not think about it in terms of building blocks. Take time to write down the things that help build confidence across the bottom of a blank page so they form a foundation layer. Then, as you experience other confidence-building scenarios, create another layer above this so you gradually form a wall. Starting from just one brick, you should eventually be able to build a cathedral of confidence.

That week at The Open certainly helped Zane build another layer of his cathedral's wall. The following week, he contested the Carris Trophy – the English Boys' Under-18 Championship – which had been all set to be the highlight of his year had it not been for his Carnoustie exploits.

And how did he fare? Well, he came third and we'll let him sum up how that felt: "I was so confident over everything in comparison with how I would have been 10 days earlier. At that event I'd have been so nervous, and all of a sudden I was up there in the lead. I think I shot 67 in the second round just to make the cut – I had a bit of a slow start but I knew I was going to make the cut. I came 3rd and was really disappointed. Yet 10 days earlier, if I'd come 3rd I'd have been ecstatic. It was a crazy turnaround in my life. My whole confidence had just changed."

Since those heady days of July 1999, Zane Scotland has not yet become a household name, even in golfing circles. He hasn't yet taken professional golf by storm and would probably now like nothing more than to stop being remembered as 'the kid who played The Open at 16'. He struggled with his game for many years, partly due to a long-term injury suffered in a car accident from which he has only recently recovered. But then midway through 2007, completely out of the blue to the casual observer, things began to change. In late June he found himself eligible for the cash-rich French Open on the main European Tour, where he contended strongly for the title until four late bogeys saw him slip to 12th place. But he still banked 65,000 euros and more importantly caught the eye of tournament organisers sufficiently to secure a number of further invites throughout late 2007. He finished 11th in the Deutsche Bank to pocket a similar amount, bringing the prospect of a full tour card firmly into view, and then sealed the deal with a hugely impressive 4th place in the British Masters.

A good finish in the lucrative Dunhill Links saw him into the top 90 on the Order of Merit, thus ensuring a full European Tour card for the very first time in 2008. Yes, it had at times looked likely that he would become one of those golfing casualties whose youthful promise might remain forever unfulfilled. But even eight years on, he's still only 25 years of age and his golfing exploits over those extraordinary two weeks in July 1999 suggest that now he has rediscovered his game, his career could well take off in the same way that Justin Rose's did once he'd finally broken through.

And regardless of what happens in the future, no-one can ever take away from Zane what he achieved at Carnoustie. One thing's for sure – the most recent changes to Open qualifying mean it will be extremely hard for other 16-year-olds to repeat the feat, so he could conceivably remain the youngest ever Open qualifier for as long as Young Tom Morris has been its youngest competitor. Goodness knows, it was an improbably tall order in 1999, which is what makes Zane's story such a remarkable one.

A routine victory

Kenneth Ferrie

Kenneth Ferrie had only been on tour a couple of years when he grabbed his first real winning chance with both hands at the 2003 Spanish Open. This story of his success that week contains little in the way of derring-do, spectacular incident or golfing perfection, but plenty of good sound advice ranging from sticking to your usual preparation and routines, to a more down-to-earth approach to frustration than you might imagine in an occasionally fiery character. And sometimes that's all winning takes.

"Before that final round I tried to keep everything the same as I do for every other round. So it was just a normal night, then I went back and watched a movie or listened to some music. I've always believed that if you're in contention and you start doing things differently then that's going to make you realise you're facing something different. It's the same on the course – whether you're four-over or four-under you should have the same routine, because that's the routine you've set for yourself."

The story of Kenneth Ferrie's progress through the professional ranks will make very familiar reading to golf followers as it's typical of the career path many fledgling pros tread. He turned pro in 1999 off a handicap of +2 and headed for the tour school at the end of that year where he was unable to make it through at the first attempt. The following year he did succeed but his first full season on the European Tour proved a bit of struggle, so at the end of 2001 he found himself back at the annual six-round qualifying marathon.

Undeterred, he comfortably played himself back on tour, and this time managed to narrowly hold on to his status at the end of the 2002 season, ending up 112th thanks mainly to a fine 3rd place finish in the French Open. There'd also been a couple of other vital top 10s during a mid-season spell of decent form that was sandwiched between a poor start and a poor end to the year. Although he had won previously on the Challenge Tour in both 2000 and 2001, that 3rd place was the first time he had really featured at the business end of a European Tour leader board, and that experience of competing perhaps proved invaluable in 2003 when his career really took a giant step forward courtesy of every young pro's ambition – a first tour title in that April's Spanish Open. This chapter is about that maiden success and what went on in Ken's mind throughout that week. But first, a little bit more about a man who is renowned for having one of the livelier on-course temperaments on the European Tour.

Ken is fully aware of his reputation and talked openly about it when asked during the 2006 US Open, where he enjoyed his best ever week in a major, playing with Phil Mickelson in the final round and eventually finishing 6th: "I wear my heart on my sleeve and that's how I play golf. That's just it. I'm sure you've got guys in America who are no different to me. Most people have a temper. It's just that some people choose to show it and other people don't. I do, unfortunately. That's part of me, and with hindsight maybe if I wasn't that way I might be a better player… and if I wasn't that way I might be a worse player. I am how I am. I keep it in check 90% of the time. I'm not perfect; nobody is. It's one of those things."

Ken admits he is never likely to find it particularly easy to instantly dismiss bad golf, going on to say: "It would be a great attitude to have – 'I've just made two double bogeys, and that isn't that bad.' Some people can do that; that's not me." But writing in The Sunday Herald in June 2006, Alasdair Reid paints a picture of a golfer who, yes, can be quick to explode, but equally, can be quick to calm back down. Reid writes: "His rounds unfold as distinctly

Montyesque soap operas, their plots lurching along a psychological rollercoaster measured by whoops of delight at their high points, and deep groans of despair in their lows. Not, it should be stressed, that he is any sort of drama queen, or that his hissy fits last more than a few moments at a time. Ferrie has been criticised for his sudden eruptions of temper, but the storms tend to blow through quickly and his composure and good grace rapidly return. Often, you will find him raging at one part of the course and beaming at another. If you're lucky, you might even see him cram his entire emotional range into one hole."

That then is the man. Now, a little more about that Spanish Open victory in April 2003. In terms of results, there had been little in the build-up to the event to suggest that a maiden win might be on the cards. The early part of the season had seen him make and miss cuts in equal measure, with a best finish of tied 16th in the previous week's Portuguese Open. Ken's week in Spain started brightly enough with a five-under par 67. But on a low scoring day that prompted Jarmo Sandelin, one of the early front-runners, to say, "if there's no 59 [this week] I would be disappointed," it was only good enough for a share of 30th place, with 143 out of 156 players on par or better at day's end.

Next day Ken shot 65 to get to 12-under, but with the halfway leaders hitting 15-under and the cut mark breaking the European Tour record at six-under, this was still only good enough for a share of 7th place. It wasn't until he repeated that score on Saturday – with eagles on both the 13th and 18th helping him cover the final 11 holes in seven-under – that Ken hit the front for the first time on 19-under, along with five other players – Paul Casey, Simon Khan, Soren Hansen, Santiago Luna and 17-year-old Spanish amateur, Pablo Martin, who would later go on to make history as the first amateur to win on the European Tour in 2007's Portuguese Open. A total of 20 players were within three shots of the lead heading into the final round, where Ken would be playing in the final group for the first time.

On that last day, the scoring frenzy eventually abated a little. Ken was hovering round the level par mark for most of the round, but when he bogeyed the 13th he wondered whether his chance had gone. But he then fought back hard with three birdies in a row from the 15th that left him needing to extend that run to four on the 72nd hole to claim the title – something very much on the cards on a straightforward par-5 that amounted to little more than a drive and a 7-iron. But it didn't happen. In fact, he ended up having to hole a gritty two-and-a-half footer for par just to join Peter Hedblom and Peter Lawrie in a play-off, where he was then, thankfully, able to make amends. After all three protagonists had made two-putt birdies first time round on that par-5 18th hole, it was Ken who hit his second shot into 12 feet next time. And although the eagle putt didn't drop, it didn't matter as neither of the two Peters could make four, leaving Ken with a simple tap-in for the trophy.

That is the tournament in a nutshell, but what exactly was going on in Ken's mind as that victorious week developed? Let's take a look at some of the key thoughts and strategies that helped him become the seventh first-time European Tour winner in just 16 events at the start of 2003.

Usual preparation

As we've read in the opening quote to this chapter, Ken is a great advocate of keeping things constant in terms of preparation, rather than forever chopping and changing in response to different situations. In that way, by the time you tee off, you'll have the reassurance of knowing everything is exactly as it always is.

That preparation can cover all sorts of things, from the time you arrive at the course, to when and how long you practise for and what you're going to do to occupy your time when you're not playing or practising. Here, Ken talks us through his preparation when it comes to pre-tournament practice rounds: "If I'm going to a golf course that I've never seen before, the first practice round is purely a recce run. It's just a case of hitting it, going round and just seeing where I'm going. The second round I use more as a proper round of golf. I don't score but I do concentrate and try and play a proper round of golf. So the first practice round is just to get the strategy – trying to get a game plan and all that – and then the second is to execute the game plan and see if that's the right way to do things."

Of course, most of us don't play practice rounds prior to the monthly Medal, but the important thing is that whatever your preparation does involve, make sure it's something you repeat before every competitive round. That way when you finally tee it up, you can do so safe in the knowledge that you've done everything you'd set yourself to do prior to the event.

When Ken was starting to turn his mind to winning a tour event in 2003, he was curious to find out whether winning entailed doing things differently, and picked Bradley Dredge's brains shortly after the Welshman had secured his maiden tour victory in Madeira. Ken remembers being reassured by Bradley's response: "He basically told me what I've told people since: 'There was nothing different that week and everything just clicked into place and felt very easy. I never once had to worry about my swing; never felt as though I was rushed; never felt as though I was going to hit a bad shot. Out of all the shots I visualised, virtually 90% of them came off absolutely inch perfect to how I'd imagined them happening.'"

Bradley hadn't changed a thing and it had worked for him, so Ken had resolved to do the same and stick to what he knew, even when he found himself in the unfamiliar territory of leading a tour event going into the final day: "I think it goes back to your preparation again. After the first three days, you've had three good rounds and you're tied for the lead of the tournament so you're obviously doing a lot of things well. So it's just a matter of relying on those things being good again." In other words, why change what is already working?

Stick to routines no matter what

Holding fast to your preparation is one thing, but what about out on the course where it can be easy to get caught up in the excitement of what's going on and forget about the specific routines you've set yourself? When you've abandoned your routine, the potential problems become twofold if something bad happens – not only have things gone wrong, but you've also probably now got a persistent little voice inside your head telling you, 'that wouldn't have happened if you'd stuck to your routine'.

Perhaps golfers can relate to this most when it comes to the putting green, and their decision over whether to putt out or mark and wait when it comes to the short ones. This usually boils down to what length putt you regard as a straightforward tap-in. The important thing is that as soon as a putt extends beyond the range you've set as your 'mark and wait' threshold, that is exactly what you must do every time – mark and wait. More apparent 'gimmes' are probably missed through breaking this routine than through any other cause. You still may not make the putt every time – after all that's why you deemed it not to be a 'gimme'. But at least if you do subsequently miss, you've only got that to deal with that and not the irritating little voice eager to further compound your frustration.

Similarly, if you have a pre-shot routine, you must see it all the way through on every shot. So if, for whatever reason, you get distracted halfway through, you must stop, step away and start the whole process again rather than trying to continue through the distraction or pick things up again midway. Ken feels that's something he does well: "You have to stick to your routines even when you're under pressure. I'm quite a finicky person and I do probably hear a lot more than most people do when I'm playing. But when I hear something like that I have to back off – that's my routine for that."

This was tested to the full when Ken stood over that short putt on the 72nd hole to get into the play-off – probably the most important one of his career. Even though it was the kind of putt he would expect to make 99 times out of 100, Ken chose to stick to his routine when an audible distraction broke his concentration: "I remember I was standing over the putt and I was just about to hit it when I heard somebody in the crowd shout out. So I actually backed off and then went back over and holed it. I think a lot of people in that situation would have been quite tempted just to hit it and get it over with regardless." Ken wasn't prepared to let a disruption to his routine affect his chances of achieving what he dearly wanted to achieve. Are we able to always say the same? Probably not.

Game plans can accommodate 'what ifs?'

Many times in this book we'll refer to the importance of setting yourself a game plan. But that's not to say it has to be 100% rigid and totally inflexible. If you'd set yourself a plan to attack regardless in an attempt to make up lost ground, and then suddenly found yourself several shots clear with a few holes to play, would it still be wise to take on the water on that par-5 or to attack the sucker pin on that dangerous par-3? Probably not, but if your game plan was purely to attack, then that's what you might feel obliged to do. But suppose you were to factor a number of 'what ifs?' into your game plan, such that if things developed in a certain way it might allow for a degree of flexibility? That's fine, as long as you come up with a solution for those 'what if?' scenarios before you tee off. For example, you might ask yourself 'what if I'm leading by three with a couple of holes to play?' And the answer might be, 'just play for a couple of safe pars so anyone chasing will have to do something pretty spectacular to catch me.' The important thing is that you rehearse and resolve each 'what if?' scenario beforehand, so you then know exactly what you're going to do if that very situation arises. It's no good leaving it until it happens before you think about it – that's when you're most likely to come up with an irrational or risky solution.

Ken liked to start looking at the scoreboards towards the end of a round when he was in contention, so that he then had a clearer picture of what he needed to do. But his overall game plan allowed for this, so in doing so he wasn't breaching the terms of his pre-round deal with himself. Ken explains: "With my first two wins on the Challenge Tour I'd said at the start of the day that I wouldn't look until near the end of the round – until the last couple of holes. The first time I looked in Spain was after I three-putted the 13th – I looked because I wanted to know where I was and what was happening. When it gets to the last four or five holes I think you need to know where you are – if you're four ahead then obviously you can be a little bit more conservative; if you're three or four behind then you may need to be a bit more aggressive." The important thing for Ken was that he'd made the decision when and where to be conservative or aggressive before he'd teed off, so when he did finally look at the leader board after 13 holes any subsequent variation in strategy wasn't breaking from his game plan so much as seeing which 'what if?' sub-clause he needed to invoke over the remaining holes.

Winning doesn't always mean great golf

One of the most important things to realise in golf is that it's still possible to score well even when certain elements of your game have gone missing. So if your ball-striking's off and you're missing greens right, left and centre, you can still get it round if your short game's on-song or your putter's on fire. Rarely do all elements of your game come together to the same degree at the same time, but it's quite possible that excelling in another area can compensate.

Ken knows only too well that the scorecard does not always reflect the quality of your play – both ways: "I've shot rounds of 64 and 65 and haven't played that well and I've shot rounds of 74 and 75 and played absolutely superbly. But people don't see that. At the end of the day you can't put your finger on it and say exactly why things happen when they do." Ken goes on to sum it all up very succinctly: "Like I say, I've played better golf since my win and actually missed cuts. If anybody could sit down and bottle what makes somebody win, they'd be very rich!"

The following year, Ken actually feels his golf improved, yet he dropped 38 places on the Order of Merit: "In 2004 I played a lot better golf. I was a lot more consistent, made more cuts and played a lot more solidly and yet I made less than half of what I'd made in 2003. But that's the thing with golf – you're only judged on your performances. People look at your scores on the internet but they don't get to see the breakdown of how you got that." At the end of that 2004 season, it appears that Ken chose to assess things based on how he felt he'd been playing rather than what the results alone appeared to suggest. So in 2005 rather than allowing himself to be tempted to start working on things he probably didn't need to work on, he simply carried on as he had been doing, even though his income had halved the previous season. Perhaps that helped contribute to an excellent 2005 in which he scooped over a million euros alone from his European Open victory and Dunhill links championship runners-up spot, ending up 11th on the Order of Merit with over 1.4 million euros in the bank.

You can't control the uncontrollable

There are many things you can control on the golf course – the quality of your ball-striking, what club you decide to hit or how well you stick to your routines. But equally there are other things which will forever remain beyond your control, however unfair it may seem – whether you get a kind or unkind bounce, whether the wind suddenly gets up after you've played leaving you in the deep front bunker, whether you get a raw deal in terms of the weather or whether, despite playing the golf of your life, someone else just happens to play even better to deny you the result you were longing for.

There are two important things to remember in all this. Firstly, there is absolutely nothing you can do about those events that are beyond your control, and secondly, that is just how golf is. If you struggle to accept that, you're going to constantly run into difficulties. Ken looks back on that play-off philosophically now, realising that things would have turned out very differently if Peter Lawrie's 15 foot eagle putt had gone in on the first play-off hole: "You can control what you do, but you can't control what others do. I won that week but if Peter Lawrie had holed that putt he would have won. You've just got to hope that when it's your week it isn't somebody else's as well." Ken knew his fate was, to a certain extent, in someone else's hands. In both scenarios, he would have played exactly the same golf, but in one he wins, and in the other he loses. So you just have to accept that you can control some things and not others, and there will be times when things beyond your control stop you getting the result you want.

Perhaps part of our problem in fully embracing this is that we now live in a world where every aspect of our lives is so precisely ordered that it's hard to accept anything is beyond our control. Ken shares his thoughts on that: "I think in modern days, in every walk of life, we're used to having everything under our control. Cars are so precise now, everything can be emailed, your banking can be done on the internet and everything can be controlled exactly the way you want it. But that's the thing with golf – it's the unknown." You probably know someone who doesn't like being a passenger in a car, far preferring to drive if given the option.

Everybody feels more comfortable when they're in control, but in golf you can only ever control a certain percentage of what happens and should always be prepared to expect the unexpected. Perhaps it might be wise to have an 80/20 rule in the back of your mind, in which you accept that you can control 80% of your score, but the remaining 20% is down to the vagaries of the game's uncontrollable factors like the luck of the bounce, a spike mark right on your line or finding your ball in a deep divot in the middle of the fairway. You can rant and rave all you like about the injustice of that 20% but it will make no difference – there is nothing you can do about it. So just accept it and make doubly sure you've done everything possible to control the things that you can control, rather than wasting time and energy worrying about the things you can't.

Handling frustrations and bad shots

You might think that given his reputation for the occasional on-course flare-up Ken would be one of those players who finds it particularly hard to cope when things go wrong or he hits bad shots. But that's not the impression you get talking to him, and he seems to have a very mature attitude off the course to the game's potential frustrations: "That's golf! I think that's the nature of the game. It's a frustrating game and it's a hard game to understand at times but I think that's its fascination and draw – that you can't master it. I think that's the thing that draws a lot of people, and I think that's also what keeps you from going mad!" After all, if the game were that easy it would quickly become boring and we'd turn to something else to provide us with the element of challenge we all desire from life.

That's not to say that bad shots don't get to Ken in their immediate aftermath. But he feels that when he does vent his anger or frustration it's all over very quickly, so that by the time he's standing over the next shot, he's ready to go again: "You get so frustrated when you hit bad shots, but I'm sure most golfers understand that if you hit bad shots and then dwell on them – keep them with you for two or three holes – it doesn't do you any good. I know it's easier said than done to be able to just click your fingers and totally get rid of the bad shot, but I think the more experience you have in golf, the more you understand that that's what you've got to do."

The perfect golfer has not yet lived and even Ben Hogan – widely acknowledged as one of the finest ball-strikers of all time – admitted to hitting just a handful of perfect shots every round. Once you get it into your head that perfection will remain forever out of reach, it can have a liberating effect on your golf. Ken has certainly been relieved to discover that even the top players fall some way short of perfection: "I've played with some of the best players in the world and they don't hit perfect golf shots. To deal with that you have to accept that you're not perfect, so your golf's not going to be perfect.

You've just got to accept that, rather than dwell on the fact, and understand that you are going to hit bad golf shots. It's the old cliché of not how but how many."

Any golfer who gets too bogged down in the quest for ultimate perfection will be in for a hard ride, because even the very best only ever achieve it a small percentage of the time.

It isn't always horses for courses

When Ken first set foot on the Costa Adeje course for his practice rounds before that 2003 Spanish Open, it didn't inspire any great hope in him for the week ahead: "Of all the golf courses that we might ever play it was probably the one I thought I couldn't win on. It was really wide open and there was no rough. My game at the time was more about hitting fairways, hitting it straight and being consistent, and that golf course was really set up for a long hitter."

But that's not a particularly helpful way of viewing things if you're a professional golfer, as you simply have to play wherever an event is being held. The record books are full of victories achieved by players whose games weren't supposed to suit certain courses, as evidenced most recently by Zach Johnson at the 2007 Masters, where, according to those in the know, only the very longest hitters now have any real chance. Fortunately Ken was able to effectively rationalise those initial thoughts: "But then what about the number of times you play a golf course that does suit you and you don't play very well? You've got to look at it that everybody who plays on tour is a good golfer and regardless of whether the course suits them or not, if they play well that week, they will have a good finish." Sometimes you have to turn things around a little in your mind to change an apparently negative outlook into a suitably positive one.

While it's never good to delude yourself, it is always far better to try and put as positive a spin as possible on any situation. So if you're heading into a tournament not playing particularly well, but not playing badly enough to warrant major swing or mind surgery, how might you go about building yourself up? Ken has a great answer to that one: "It's the old one about trying to kid yourself that if you're a good golfer and you haven't been playing well for a few days, eventually you are going to start playing well. And if you're going to start playing well why can't it be at the start of this tournament? That's the golfer, or sportsman, thinking about it logically. When you sit down and think about it, it doesn't make sense for a streak to last forever. When it's a good streak you think it can, but when it's a bad streak you expect it to end very soon. It's trying to find a positive way of looking at it both ways."

Don't get ahead of yourself

Ken got a stark reminder during his Spanish Open win about the dangers of getting ahead of yourself and mentally awarding yourself the victory before you've crossed the finishing line. After his little birdie treble from the 15th to the 17th Ken did a bit of premature chicken counting, taking the birdie he needed to win up the easy par-5 18th rather too much for granted. He can laugh about it now, but it probably seemed less amusing at the time. Ken recalls: "I got a little bit ahead of myself. My caddy and I always have a bit of a laugh because he remembers when I holed the putt at 17, I was walking round like I'd just made three in a row, and I just walked up to him and said, 'Jimmy, I've won!' We always have a laugh about that because I got a bit ahead of myself. Standing on the last tee, I had to birdie the hole to win the tournament – a hole that I hit driver, 7-iron into in the play-off. But I actually had to scramble to make par just to get into the play-off – I had to hole about a two-footer for par."

It really is very important to leave any celebrating until after the final shot has been struck. Every club golfer will be able to remember a time when he was mentally celebrating a win or handicap cut, only for the wheels to fall off with a few holes to go. And most will also have a tale of last-hole woe to tell, that, like Ken, they can laugh about now, but at the time probably seemed like the end of their golfing world.

And it's not just us. While no-one is suggesting he was congratulating himself prematurely at the 1999 Open, Jean van de Velde could probably have been excused for doing so needing just a double bogey to clinch the Claret Jug – and we all know what happened next! And those with longer memories may recall Arnold Palmer walking up the final hole of the 1961 Masters to wild applause and much congratulatory back-slapping from friends on his third Green Jacket in four years. His drive had split the fairway leaving a simple 7-iron in for the par that would seal victory. A simple 7-iron? He came off the shot slightly ending up in the right-hand bunker, caught his attempted splash shot slightly thin sending his ball over the green and down the far slope, decided to putt back up the slope on the grounds that your worst putt is always better than your worst chip, ran it 15 feet by and missed the return. That double bogey from a seemingly invincible position meant that it was Gary Player's chest measurements Masters officials were calling for ahead of the prize ceremony rather than Arnold's. So just remember – it's never over till it's over.

Mixed emotions

Before that final round Ken had to deal with one or two mixed emotions about the day ahead – caught somewhere between wanting to win, and not wanting to embarrass himself. Ken recalls: "It was a bit of a mixed thing to be brutally honest. You've got half of you thinking, 'right, let's go out, have a really good day and win,' and the other half thinking, 'just don't have a bad round; don't make a fool of yourself.'" His play during the final round suggests that he'd probably managed to focus much more on the former, as the latter, understandable though it may be, is far more likely to result in you breaking away from the very attitudes that have helped get you in contention in the first place.

After Ken had done well enough to make the play-off, again it was a time for slightly mixed emotions, but this time in a way that probably helped take the pressure off a little as he faced the most important golf holes of his life. Yes, he knew that it was a real opportunity to win, but he also knew that whatever happened, he had already achieved one of his key goals for the season with his guaranteed runners-up spot. Ken explains: "That was my third year on tour, and early in the year one of the main goals for somebody in my situation is just to secure your card as soon as you can. I'd already made about 30 or 40 grand that year so I knew that getting in the play-off was enough to reach that goal. My thinking was that one of my main goals for the year has been achieved – anything else is a bonus. That kind of takes the pressure off a bit."

Yes, winning is ultimately what professional golfers are trying to do, but you can only do that if you're actually out on tour. Ken was able to rationalise things such that even before the play-off he knew he'd already achieved a key goal for the year, so he'd be able to take something positive away from the week regardless.

The beauty of this attitude was that it took the fear out of the new situation Ken was facing. After all, what was the worst that could happen? He'd lose the play-off but still make more than enough to achieve one of his goals for the year with the season little more a third of the way through. Ken admits that to some this may not seem like the ideal way of looking at it, and ahead of that play-off remembers saying to himself: "'If I do win it'll be lovely, but if I don't I've still had a good week here.' Maybe that's not the attitude to have to win tournaments, and it's a bit of a false confidence you're giving yourself that you've had a good week regardless..." Maybe, but then if one of his key goals was to secure his card as early as possible in the season, and he was guaranteed to achieve that whatever happened in the play-off, that would still be a huge positive to take away from the week even if the win eluded him. Either way, it was certainly enough to help him approach those crucial extra holes in a more relaxed frame of mind.

We hope this chapter has helped counter any initial concerns you may have had as to whether a player like Kenneth Ferrie, who self-admittedly wears his heart on his sleeve, can possibly teach you anything about mental toughness. Yes, he does sometimes flare up on the course, but he also believes that he's always back in control in time to execute the next shot free from the negative vibes of that initial reaction. And away from the course he has adopted an extremely philosophical approach to the game's many potential frustrations. You'd do well to do the same, especially if an inability to cope with them is the one thing that's really holding you back.

Star pupil

Richard McEvoy

In 2003, former Walker Cup player and rookie pro, Richard McEvoy, enjoyed a good year on the Challenge Tour, but not quite good enough to earn his full European Tour card. So come November he headed off to the annual qualifying school in Spain, not with the feelings of trepidation that seem to burden so many of his colleagues ahead of this demanding six-round ordeal, but rather a real desire not just to get his card, but to actually win the event. And he did just that. Here's the story of his week.

"Yes, I felt I had a strong chance to go out and win. I'd played great golf that year and had so many top 10s, but the only thing I hadn't done was to win a tournament. So I thought, 'just go out, forget everything else, forget the year just gone – this is the start of a new year. Go out, try your best and see what happens.'"

Tour qualifying school – or Q-school – takes place at the end of every season, with scores of golfers either battling it out for a place on the cash-rich European Tour for the first time, or seeking to regain their playing privileges after a season or more of poor form that has seen them languishing outside the all-important top 115 on the Order of Merit.

For many, though not all, this gruelling six-round examination is pretty much the closest you can get to legalised torture – an event they look forward to about as eagerly as a trip to the dentist for root canal surgery. Even those who subsequently go on to enjoy success at a much higher level in the game sometimes cite those dreaded Q-school weeks as the toughest of their careers.

Why should that be when, on the face of it at least, it's just another golf tournament? Simple really – that single week determines exactly where – if anywhere – they'll get the chance to play for their livings the following year. The ultimate prize is a place on the European Tour and the chance to compete for millions and millions of euros, so there's an awful lot resting on one week's performance. The stakes are high, and as a consequence, it's a place where you can almost smell the fear of failure.

It's also a place that pits opposite ends of golf's experience spectrum directly against each other in the battle for full tour status. Aspiring young players know that it's their form on that one week rather than how well they've been playing all season that will determine their immediate golfing future. The old guard who have lost their cards through either poor form, or an increasingly tough struggle to keep pace with the modern power game, know that everything they've lived and breathed for so long could suddenly be taken away if they don't perform that week, leaving them facing either demotion or unemployment next season. Not surprisingly, nearly everyone is feeling it during that long November week.

German golfer, Alex Cejka, chose to put himself through it not once, but twice in 2006, playing in the Q-schools for both the European and PGA Tours almost back to back in an attempt to cover all options for 2007. After successfully regaining his cards on both sides of the Atlantic, a relieved Cejka said, "I'm just glad it's over. It's been a long month for me. I did Q-school in Europe two weeks ago and now here. Now I think I am going to go throw up!" Perhaps rather too graphic a reminder of just what state the whole experience can leave even seasoned professionals in.

But that isn't quite how Richard McEvoy viewed Q-school. He'd enjoyed a very successful final year as an amateur in 2001, winning the Lytham Trophy and Irish Amateur Championship in consecutive weeks, before being selected for the Walker Cup squad that comfortably defended the trophy at Sea Island, Georgia in August. After returning to Britain to play in the Home Internationals, Richard joined the professional ranks, but didn't get past stage one of that year's Q-school after what he calls a "shocking" last round at Chart Hills in Kent. He did notch up a couple of wins on the lesser EuroPro Tour the following year, but made little impact in the rare starts he was granted on the Challenge Tour and main European Tour. So at the end of 2002 it was back to Q-school once more.

This time he got through to the final stages in Spain, and although he didn't quite do well enough to secure a full tour card he did end up with a good exemption category for the second tier Challenge Tour. A solid but ultimately winless season left him in 19th place there at the end of 2003, missing out on automatic promotion to the European Tour by just four places and little over 8,000 euros. So once again it was back to Q-school, but because of the good season he'd just enjoyed and the experience he'd gained from his previous visits, he wasn't approaching it with the same apprehension as many of his fellow competitors. Richard explains: "I felt great. I'd played great all year. I was obviously very, very disappointed not to get my card through the Challenge Tour, but my game was still in great shape and I was still playing good golf. I'd played great all year and so I was looking forward to going to tour school and doing well there." Armed with such positive pre-tournament feelings, it's perhaps little surprise that Richard's week at Emporda and Platja de Pals on the Costa Brava turned into such a successful, and ultimately victorious one for him.

The week started pretty tamely with an opening 72 that saw him down in 106th place eight shots off the pace. But Richard wasn't unduly concerned as he felt he'd played well but simply been caught wielding a stone-cold putter. The putter warmed up a little the next day, and although a solid second round 66 meant he was still eight shots off the pace, he was now comfortably inside the top 40.

Then things began to happen just as Richard had been hoping, and indeed expecting them to. Scores of 67 and 65 in the third and fourth rounds got him within four shots of Francois Delamontagne's lead and right on course for one of the 35 full tour cards on offer, before a blistering fifth round 63 took him to the head of affairs. Time to back off and just make sure of securing one of those precious cards in the final round perhaps? That wasn't how Richard approached it, and not just because it had been his intention before the event to win it rather than just get through it. Richard explains: "Yes, it was probably one of the best rounds of golf I'd ever played. And no, I wasn't under much pressure because I was already in the zone of getting my card. But on the other hand, the higher up you finish at tour school the better the card you get for the following year. So rather than just finishing in the top 35 I was still looking to win."

So Richard teed off on that final day with a three-shot lead but no thoughts of just trying to hold on. Instead, because he knew he was playing well, he just carried on doing the same things he'd been doing all week, trusting that the birdies would come as they had done only too readily once his putter had kicked into gear. Richard sums up his attitude ahead of that final round: "The scoring was so low all week I knew that even with a three-shot lead I needed to shoot three-, four- or five-under to win. I'd shot eight-under on the fifth day so I knew other people could go out and shoot eight-, nine- or 10-under. But I just had so much confidence because I'd played so well all week and knew how good my game was at the time. I knew that I could make a load more birdies still, so it didn't really bother me that people might shoot a low score because I knew I could go out and do exactly the same. If I went out and shot four- or five-under, then they'd have had to shoot eight- or nine-under to beat me – that was the only way."

When Richard closed with a 67 to meet his side of this bargain, and his closest challengers were unable to produce the magic they needed, his three-shot lead remained intact and he had graduated from Q-school with top honours and a staggering 28-under par total. He had teed off in the six-round marathon feeling confident enough in his game to be eyeing up victory, and gone on to achieve that very goal in the face of stiff opposition. So what else apart from confidence helped him through a week that makes or breaks so many careers every year? Over the following pages we'll take a look at some of the ways in which Richard feels mental strength helped him achieve his Q-school goals.

Same again please

Sometimes when we approach a big event or one we really want to do well in, we make the mistake of changing our preparation and routine simply because we feel we ought to – even if what we've been doing has been working very nicely. We'd do well to heed Manchester United manager, Alex Ferguson's, advice here – "play the game, not the occasion." In other words, keep doing the things you normally do. Instead, we often allow ourselves to be tempted into intensifying our practice regimes, or arriving at the course considerably earlier than usual on the day of the competition because we've convinced ourselves that's what's needed to meet the new challenge we face. But often it has just the opposite effect because it gets us out of our successful routines, and merely serves to emphasise in our minds that we're breaking new ground.

The 2003 Q-school was an extremely important event for Richard because it would determine when and where he would get to play in 2004. But despite this he made sure he kept his preparation exactly the same as normal, as he explains here: "I think that if you practise harder for a bigger tournament it doesn't work. You need to have a routine – a routine preparation of getting up at a certain time and doing all the normal things that you'd do for a normal tournament. Sometimes it's good to peak at a certain time, but I think you can only do that through doing exactly the same as you've always done, with perhaps just a few bits and pieces here and there that might need slightly adjusting."

Richard had also found his first full year as a travelling tournament professional quite a long one so the last thing he needed to be doing was upping the workload ahead of what would now be the most important week of the year for him. Richard remembers: "With all the travelling and everything that comes with it I had found it quite a tiring year so I think I took a week off and then just practised like I would for any normal tournament. I didn't make any specific changes for the tour school." This was undoubtedly the right thing for Richard to do. Tiger Woods has said that peaking for a tournament is simply a matter of being as physically and mentally fresh as possible, which means that, if anything, you should consider decreasing your workload rather than increasing it.

When it comes to the biggest events, if what you've been doing in terms of preparation has been delivering the goods, you're far better off sticking with it rather than introducing unfamiliar and time-consuming new elements into your pre-tournament routine.

Confidence and determination

The 2003 season had at first left Richard with mixed feelings – disappointment that he hadn't quite managed to secure his full tour card via his Challenge Tour ranking, but satisfaction that he had played well and put together a decent series of results in his first full year, including seven top 10s. Rather than dwelling on the former, Richard chose to focus on the latter as he prepared for Q-school, which meant he was able to approach the event in a confident, determined way: "I had a lot of confidence in myself to do well, and other people around me had a lot of confidence in me to do well at the same time, which I think brought the confidence out in me even more. I was definitely up for doing really well and making a lot of birdies that week, and that's what I did. I just went out and attacked the golf courses."

Richard had also had to sit back and watch as a number of friends progressed up to the main tour, and he used that as a motivating force too. Firstly because if he was on the Challenge Tour and they were on the European Tour then he wouldn't get to see them that often and secondly because he felt he was every bit as good as them. Richard describes the impact that had on his mood prior to Q-school: "Seeing a lot of my friends getting their cards through the Challenge Tour just made me even more determined to go out and do well at tour school. I'd probably played the most consistent golf out of anyone on the Challenge Tour that year and I knew I should have been one of the top 15 really but just hadn't quite done it. I knew my game was in shape and I knew all I wanted to do was just go out and get my card, and I wasn't fazed by the fact that I'd been there twice before and hadn't done it."

Richard had a choice as to where to channel his thoughts. He could have wallowed in the negatives of narrowly missing out on automatic promotion from the Challenge Tour or his two previous Q-school failures, but chose instead to think only about the positives – he'd enjoyed a good season, his game was in good shape, and he believed he was as good as any of his friends who were about to move up a level. So going into a tournament where he knew many players would be struggling to fend off negative emotions, Richard opted to entertain only positive, confident thoughts about the week ahead.

Nothing to lose; everything to gain

Richard felt that because his Challenge Tour ranking from 2003 had at least ensured him a full season there again in 2004, it had given him a safety net that meant he probably had less to potentially lose at Q-school than many others taking part. There would be players there for whom failure to secure a tour card would leave them scratching around on the mini-tours or back in the pro shop again the following season, while others – like Ryder Cup hero Philip Walton – were facing the prospect of effectively losing their jobs after a number of years.

Richard reasoned that the latter type of player – in harsh but fair terms, someone on their way down – had at least as much to lose as they did to gain.

If they didn't play well enough to get their card back, what would they do next year – try and get by on a handful of starts in mainly lesser events or resign themselves to going back to the tours from whence they'd come many years earlier? Not many are really prepared to do that after playing at the top level for so long. But Richard was guaranteed a full year's competitive golf on the Challenge Tour in 2004 even if he didn't get through Q-school, and feels that rationalising it in this way proved extremely beneficial: "I thought some people had got a lot more to lose than they had to gain really, whereas because I was young, I'd got everything in front of me. So I thought that if I were to miss my card it wouldn't be the end of the world as I'd be back on the Challenge Tour where I'd got a great category. I'd play another season there, where I'd played so well that year, and just go out and get my card through the Challenge Tour. Thinking about it in that way took a lot of pressure off me."

While your initial response to this may be that it sounds like a slightly defeatist or self-preserving attitude, Richard was actually using it to boost his confidence yet further ahead of a competition in which anything that can relieve the pressure in even a small way can only ever be a good thing.

Beware the sick or wounded golfer

If you look back at tour events over the years, it's surprising just how often flu-ridden players have come to the fore when you might have expected just the opposite – hence the above phrase. Quite why that should be isn't 100% certain. Maybe it's because they're having to devote so much of their energy to simply getting their bodies fit that there's less scope to worry about other things. Equally it may simply be that it prevents them from overdoing things in practice, because they're simply not physically capable of doing too much.

Obviously this isn't something you have any control over in your preparation, but Richard does feel a pre-tournament bout of flu that forced him to delay his flight out to Spain helped ease certain pressures that week: "I think because

I was ill it took a lot of pressure off me. They do say 'beware the injured golfer' and I think it just helped me relax. I wasn't on best form with my body and everything so I just got on with it and didn't really worry about anything."

It also made doubly sure that he wouldn't be changing his routine by upping his practice levels because his body simply wouldn't have tolerated it, even if the temptation had been there. Richard describes just how the flu had left him feeling: "I hardly went out in the evenings at all that week. I didn't really do anything because I was so tired all the time. I warmed up before going out to play and warmed down slightly afterwards as I always do. But I didn't do as much as normal, and then went straight back to the apartment and relaxed because that was what I needed to do." Tournament golf can be extremely demanding even when you're feeling as fit as a fiddle so it's always wise to conserve energy whenever possible.

A different kind of week

Ensuring that you don't overdo things, thus risking spreading yourself too thinly, is perhaps even more important during Q-school week because the very nature of the event means it can be much more physically demanding than most weeks, even before you factor in the pressure that most players are feeling. It's six rounds rather than the normal four, and it's usually played over two different courses. So by the time you've practised adequately over both, that's quite an intensive period of non-stop golf in a highly competitive environment.

Richard's experience of Q-school from the previous year meant he was well aware of this, so he knew just how important it would be to pace himself accordingly throughout the week: "I don't think it's a stressful week, but I just know how long a week it can end up being because obviously six rounds of golf is a lot, plus all your practice as well. You're playing eight or nine rounds of golf and you don't get a day off, so you need to take it easy. You can't go out and grind and hit balls for three or four hours after you've played or anything like that. You've got to conserve your energies because it's a very, very long week."

Again it's back to what constitutes ideal preparation. While it's always wise not to go beyond your normal routine ahead of any event, it's even more important when that event places greater demands on you than normal. But they're also usually the very events where the temptation to do more is greatest simply because of their significance. Richard knew exactly what to expect that week, so wouldn't have been tempted to overdo things even before his ailing body had ruled out that possibility. But equally, we need to be in control of our minds enough not to start tinkering with our routines even when the body is more than willing.

Being philosophical and patient

Bad starts don't always lead to bad endings and there's always plenty of time to recover in a 72-hole event let alone a 108-hole competition. For proof of this, look no further than the 1997 Masters, where a young Tiger Woods played his first nine holes in an error-strewn 40 strokes, before coming back in a spectacular 30 for an opening 70. Three days later, after tacking scores of 66, 65 and 69 onto that opening effort, he'd broken the 18-hole Masters scoring record and run out the winner by an incredible 12 shots – another Tiger record unlikely to be broken any time soon!

So perhaps one of the most important things Richard did that week was not to panic when a first round 72 got him off to a less than ideal start. He was able to rationalise that even though the score hadn't been what he would have wanted, he still felt he had played well tee-to-green and had simply been betrayed by a disobedient putter. Richard was able to adopt a philosophical approach that kept a potentially disappointing result in perspective, rather than letting it trigger an unnecessary and irrational reaction. He knew that the score on the card doesn't always reflect the quality of your play and it's vital not to let your reaction to such rounds get out of hand: "Yes, they're just very frustrating days. You can go out one day, rip the stick out and only shoot two- or three-under and then the next day, you don't play great golf, hole everything in sight and walk off the golf course feeling as if you haven't even played that well and yet you've shot five- or six-under. And you think 'well, how's that fair?' But golf works like that unfortunately. That's just what it's like and you've just got to get used to it being like that."

Every golfer who's ever played the game will be able to remember days when they've ended up with far more than they've seemingly deserved, and others where they've walked off with the very worst score they could possibly have shot given the quality of their ball-striking. Often – though not always – it simply comes down to whether or not the putter behaves. That's certainly how Richard felt that week in Spain, and it was the main reason why he refused to be unduly alarmed when things didn't happen in the first round. He knew he was playing well and that it was just a matter of waiting for the putter to catch up with the rest of his game, which it duly did from the following day to the final round.

Patience wins over panic every time on the golf course, especially as sometimes events beyond your control dictate whether your ball stays on the fairway or runs into a bunker, for instance. Richard knows that only too well: "Golf is very much a patience game. You've got to keep very, very patient. Sometimes it goes right for you, sometimes it doesn't. The thing about golf is you can't control a lot of things that happen to your golf ball – maybe there's a little bump on the green that makes the difference between your ball going in and not going in. But the next day you might hit a bad putt and it will go in because it hits the bump on the other side. So it's just very much a game of patience."

Patience is a vital quality to possess in your efforts to stick to any game plan you've set yourself because it means you're less likely to be lured away from it when things don't seem to be going your way. Conversely, impatience is definitely one to cross off your wish list on the course because as soon as something seems to go against you, you'll be far more likely to react to it than simply accept it as part and parcel of the game. Good bounces happen, bad bounces happen – and you can't actually do anything about either. So be patient enough to accept the latter as readily as you do the former. Any other reaction has the power to harm the rest of your round.

Detailed stats don't lie

Statistics may have the unfortunate reputation of being the next step on from lies and damned lies, but that is to do them a grave disservice in the golfing context. Richard is heavily into his stats so knew that everything else was pretty much in place that week and it was just a matter of waiting for his putter to show up: "I knew I was playing well because I'd been doing my stats every evening, and when I do my stats I can see that I'm playing well by the amount of greens and fairways I'm hitting in regulation. On the second day when I started putting really well, I knew I was going to have a good week because my game was on. So I knew something was going to happen but didn't quite know I was going to end up 28-under!"

Sometimes you'll know exactly where any problems lie without having to resort to statistics, but at other times the picture can be a little bit hazier. For example, is the root problem really that you're not putting well or rather that you're simply not hitting your approach shots close enough to generate realistic birdie opportunities? The more detailed you make your stats the clearer the picture that will begin to emerge as a result. Richard knew from the stats he was keeping that a cold putter was only partly to blame for his mediocre first round: "My stats are very, very detailed so I can see exactly how close, or how far away I'm hitting it. If you're good at it, you can usually see what you've done wrong and what you haven't done wrong when you come off the golf course. But if you're writing it down, then it's there in front of you. It doesn't lie. So you can't tell yourself you've had a bad putting day if you're hitting it to 30 feet on every green. That's no good because you can't expect to hole 30-footers all the time. For me, it's usually a matter of just hitting the ball in closer with my shorter irons, which is what I did that week – that's why I ended up being on top."

Have you ever tried keeping detailed stats about your game? You may have dismissed it as being a bit too geeky for you, but if you're serious about improving it can be one of the best ways of ensuring that the route you take going forwards is the most direct one rather than a confusing detour. Richard's putter got going from the second round onwards, but he feels that this was probably as a direct result of him hitting it closer more often – exactly what his stats had suggested was most required. The beauty of stats is that they present evidence in a totally objective way completely devoid of muddled subjectivity. As a result they can force you to face up to things you've either simply been unaware of or have perhaps been trying to run away from.

Hard work pays off

Richard's stats had shown that to have a better chance of shooting lower scores he needed to be hitting his shorter irons close enough to create real birdie chances. That had been one of the main things he had worked on throughout that year, so it was extremely gratifying for him to be able to reap the dividends of all his endeavours when it most counted. Richard certainly feels that that's what happened: "What I remember most about that week was that my wedge-play was fantastic. I'd worked hard on my wedge-play all year but it hadn't really come together yet. But my distance control and my wedge-play were just fantastic that week. That's why I made so many birdies I think, because I had the ball in the right place so many times. And if you keep hitting it in close, eventually it's going to happen and the putts are going to drop, and I think that's what happened that week really." Sometimes you don't reap the rewards of hard work straightaway, but the important thing is that if you feel that what you're working on is right, you have to keep persevering in the belief that eventually all your efforts will pay off. It certainly did for Richard that week.

Stretch yourself

Richard set himself performance goals that week which he felt were achievable, but which would also push him a little. For example, he was trying to hit it closer with his short irons because he knew that was an area of his game where there was real room for improvement. But he was careful not to make his goals too specific in terms of scores: "I don't think you set yourself a particular score to go out and shoot but you do set yourself a certain thing to do for that day – maybe to try and move up to a certain position in the field or, like I said, hit it closer to the hole. It's not really about the score although you might have one in the back of your mind. But it's not a specific score where you say 'I've got to shoot 66 tomorrow and if I don't shoot that then I won't have achieved my goal.' That's not a proper kind of goal because you could go out and shoot 67 and still win, but you wouldn't have reached your goal. What's the point in that? So I think you've got to make them broad and you've got to set goals that will realistically make you a better player."

If specific outcome goals are one thing to avoid, then so too are ones that are too easy to achieve. If the former are prone to leaving you dissatisfied more often than satisfied, then the latter serve no real purpose at all. If you're looking to improve, yet your performance goals are only ever based on what you're already capable of, then you're not going to be stretching yourself enough. Richard certainly feels that way: "You should set your goals higher rather than lower as – more than anything – you need something to push you on. If you're setting your goals at a medium level and you're not pleased once you've reached those goals, then I don't think they were really high enough. Sometimes you've got to set yourself high goals to achieve what you want to achieve."

It's all about pitching your performance goals at the right level. Too high and you're likely to become demoralised as all you ever encounter is apparent failure; too low, and although in relation to your goals you might be succeeding, your actual progress will be minimal because they clearly haven't been demanding enough to take you beyond the level you're already at. If you're not sure what kind of performance goals to set yourself take a look at some of the statistical categories on the European Tour's website for some ideas – things like the number of fairways you hit, number of greens you hit in regulation, the percentage of times you get up and down from the sand, or how many putts you're averaging. Then work out what would constitute sufficient improvement in one or all of these categories to take those elements of your game to the next level.

As we've already said, one of Richard's chief goals that week was to hit his short irons closer than he had been doing, so he was understandably delighted with his final approach shot of the tournament. We'll let Richard take up the story: "The thing that really sticks in my mind was my third shot over water into the par-5 last hole. I'd hit a poor tee shot and chipped out of the trees. I had a 9-iron in my hands, and my third shot hit the pin which just summed up my whole week really because what I'd aimed to do that week was to go out and hit the ball in closer. So to hit the pin on the last hole and finish like that – you know, a foot away – just rounded off the week and highlighted how well I had achieved that goal."

At that point in Richard's career everything seemed to be falling into place relatively easily, placing little strain on his powers of patience. As Richard said at the time: "I'm lucky enough that I haven't had to be very patient really. On a golf course obviously you have to be very patient with regard to making birdies or making putts or what have you. But with regard to setting your goals and reaching those goals I haven't had to be very patient. I've literally set myself goals that I've reached really quickly, so I've been lucky in that sense."

Either lucky, or perhaps more likely, sensible enough to set his goals at an achievable level.

Since then his patience has probably been tested a little more as he has so far struggled to really establish himself on the full European Tour. At the time of writing Richard was still engaged in a see-saw battle to fully make the transition from Challenge Tour to European Tour. He failed to keep his card at the end of 2004 and went back to the Challenge Tour in 2005, where he won the second event of the season before ending up 10th on the end-of-year Order of Merit to once again regain his full tour status. But he was then unable to make the top 115 on the 2006 Order of Merit, necessitating another trip to Q-school where once again he got his card back for the main tour.

The road to success is a long, hard journey for all players and one that should never be abandoned too hastily because the nature of the game means that time really is on your side much more than in many sports. If you want a little inspiration take a look at Ian Woosnam, Mike Weir and Tom Lehman who all endured several visits to tour school before finally breaking through and ultimately going on to become major champions. Lehman was well into his 30s before he was able to establish himself as a world class player on the PGA Tour in 1992. So as Richard strives to establish himself on the European Tour, now more than ever is the time not to panic, but rather to hold on to that philosophical, patient approach that served him well enough at 2003's Q-school to finish the week as its star pupil.

60 to win

Jamie Spence

Few golfers claim their maiden tour victories in quite such spectacular fashion as Jamie Spence. In 1992 he started the final round of the European Masters 10 strokes adrift and three hours ahead of leader, Colin Montgomerie. Yet just 60 shots and eight hours later he was clutching the trophy. So what factors helped Jamie start low, then just keep going lower on that remarkable Sunday?

"I thought on the par-5 14th, 'I've got a chance here' because I knew that I was playing well. I birdied that one down the hill, and then we turned up the hill and I thought, 'we've got to have a go at this par-5.' I hit two great shots onto the green, then holed the putt from about 30 feet for an eagle, and when that went in I thought, 'I can win this now.' At that point I really thought, 'right, now I can win.'"

Shooting 60 in a European Tour event is incredibly rare with only a dozen or so players ever managing to achieve it and no-one ever bettering it. Doing it in the last round to win is rarer still. Only two have managed that. And shooting 12-under par in the final round to claim your maiden tour title narrows the list down to just one – Jamie Spence in the suitably fairytale-like setting of the Swiss Alps in the 1992 European Masters. For the record, Ian Woosnam was the other last round 60-shooting winner in the 1990 Monte Carlo Open over a par-69 course.

At the point of the round Jamie had reached in our opening quote he still had three holes to play, and yet somehow he already felt as though he was going to win. As it transpired, if he hadn't gone on to birdie the final three holes as his pièce de resistance, he wouldn't have done. But just what gave him the belief that he could pull it off with so many other golfers barely into their rounds that day? In a moment, we'll look back with Jamie at that remarkable last round, but before that, a little of his career history as a professional to put things in context.

Like any aspiring pro, Jamie wanted to play on the big stage. After turning pro in 1985 he decided he would give himself five goes at getting his tour card via the qualifying school, and succeeded in making it through in 1986 and 1989. His first full year on tour in 1987 proved largely unfruitful, but in 1990 he was able to finally establish himself as a tour player, thanks in no small measure to a 3rd place finish in the same European Masters where he would go on to shoot that final round 60 just two years later. That 1990 season kicked off a 15-year unbroken spell as a full tour cardholder for Jamie.

In early 1990 Jamie had started to feel more comfortable on tour and his results began to reflect that. Then in that year's Open at St Andrews – Jamie's first – he made a big breakthrough. He didn't win, nor did he finish in the top 10. But after blasting his way near the top of the 2nd round leader board with a 65, he did go on to make the top 25 and convince himself that he was good enough to be out on tour. Looking back to 1990, Jamie recalls that his goals changed from simply wanting to stay out on tour to something far more ambitious: "After that season, I just thought, 'let's try and get out there and win an event.' And that became my main focus."

He began to blossom into first a good player, and then a very good player – 51st on the Order of Merit in 1990, 29th in 1991, and then the winning breakthrough of 1992. He was in the middle of a good season, had started reasonably well in the European Masters, but had then shot himself out of it with a one-over par 73 on Saturday to fall 10 shots behind 3rd round leader, Colin Montgomerie.

But on Sunday he played like a man possessed, racking up 10 birdies, an eagle and no bogeys to surge past a faltering Monty – and everyone else for that matter – closing out the round by playing the final five holes in six-under par. Then when Anders Forsbrand had the audacity to birdie the last five holes to force a tie, he kept his nerve to win at the second play-off hole, again birdieing the 18th.

This chapter looks at some of the things that helped put Jamie in a position where he really felt he was good enough to win, before going on to see exactly what went on in his mind as that magical final round unfolded.

The learning curve

For all but the most talented, it's invariably true that to win you first have to lose. Fresh-on-tour golfers arrive in an arena far-removed from the amateur circuit, regional tournaments, or the lesser tours. Jamie remembers those early days when his golfing idols became no longer just people he watched on the telly, but fellow tour pros standing next to him on the range: "It was a learning curve. Teeing up on the practice ground with Seve and Faldo and those guys in their prime – it was very intimidating."

Every new golfing environment requires a period of adjustment, whether it's the tour or starting to compete alongside golfers you've always looked up to at your club. Later on there may be another learning curve when you become proficient enough to start knocking on the door in tournaments. Jamie remembers one or two near misses in the time between that 1990 Open and his eventual victory in Switzerland: "Like a lot of guys trying to win their first events, you get very close. But when you're up there playing with the top players, the slightest mistake costs you." In the Austrian Open a couple of months before his victory, Jamie raced through the field with a final round 63. But a shortish birdie putt on the 18th refused to drop, and when Peter Mitchell chipped in on the same hole for eagle, another one had gone astray by the narrowest of margins. Jamie recalls: "I was close again, but if you've got four guys belting it out someone's going to do something remarkable like chipping in, and Pete did it." Little did he know that a couple of months later he'd be doing something much more remarkable to clinch his first victory.

Wise players store these experiences away for the future. In the European Masters two years earlier, Jamie had learned a lot from playing with eventual winner, Ronan Rafferty. Teeing off in the final Sunday pairing for the first time, Jamie didn't disgrace himself, finishing 3rd. But he did watch and learn too, noting that winning rarely requires perfect golf: "I realised playing with him that you haven't got to hit the ball fantastically well all the way round. Ronan was a great thinker round the course and he hit his irons very well. And I realised that you've got to hit your medium-short irons well. You've got to get them close, which is what he did. But he took all the shots on as well. When I had chances in the next couple of years, I'd learned a lot from that experience."

For every golfer who enjoys instant success when moving up a level, 100 others have to graft it out over a longer period. So unless you're especially talented don't hold impatient or unrealistic ambitions when breaking new ground – it will probably take a while to feel comfortable there.

The confidence factor

Despite our best attempts to constantly build up our confidence levels, we are still likely to encounter times when it is a willing accomplice and others when it seems but a distant memory. Don't spurn its benefits when it's in town. There's nothing wrong with it as long as there are sound reasons for it and you don't stray into the land of overconfidence. Jamie certainly played with confidence in the early part of 1992: "I was just riding a crest. I was playing well all that year really and just kept going. It's like most of the guys you see – you just keep going. You don't want to get off that wave of confidence."

There'll probably be other times when confidence is but a distant memory. So if you're playing well, feed off it for a while and see where it leads. This will be far easier if you adopt an attitude that says 'I'm playing well at the moment so expect to do well next time I tee it up,' rather than one that says, 'I'm playing well, but I know it can't last. Perhaps this round will be the one where it all goes wrong.'

In the early 1990s, Jamie adopted the former approach, and with good reason – his play and results justified it. He remembers: "At that point in my golf, if I got on a course that was set up like the one in Switzerland, I could shoot low numbers. I really could. My short iron-play was such that I could hit it close, and I could putt. I could hole lots of putts." And of that particular round of 60: "I knew I was capable of it – it wasn't a shock to shoot that score. Since then I've got into some positions where I've shot good scores and sort of expected it too."

Never deny yourself confidence in your golf if the foundations on which your game is built justify it as they did for Jamie at that particular stage of his career.

Just relax

On Saturday night in Switzerland, Jamie thought his winning chances were over, which in itself may have helped him achieve what he did the following day. He certainly feels that way: "On the last hole of the third round I three-putted for bogey and thought that was that. My wife Sally was with me and we went back to the hotel and had a couple of bottles of wine and I just relaxed really and thought 'well, that's another one gone, I'll think about the next one.' I think what happened was I relaxed a lot and just allowed myself to play."

That last comment is the critical one – 'allowed myself to play' – because all too often when golfers are in contention, they tense up mentally and physically, and simply don't allow themselves to play. In a perverse way, by shooting himself out of the tournament, Jamie had effectively shot himself back into it. He wasn't thinking about winning, but certainly hadn't stopped trying: "I thought if I could shoot 66 or 65 maybe I'd make top 10. So I'd not given up by any stretch. But I was certainly more relaxed than I would have been if I'd been up there. I knew there was a low score on because it was a beautiful day, and then I went out in five-under." Still no real pressure at this point as Jamie was simply playing for a high finish, rather than even entertaining thoughts about winning – those would first surface a few holes later, giving him another four or so holes to play in relaxed freedom.

Many average golfers' career-best nine holes directly follow front nines of pure disaster. They stop striving once 'the score' is gone, and suddenly find themselves able to play. It's the same on tour, and one reason why the majority of very low scores come from players off the pace. Jamie sums it up: "It's easier, isn't it? You don't see too many guys shooting 61s and 62s when they're leading or one off the lead because they're caught up in the crowd and the expectation, and the nerves are there from the first tee. It's far easier to shoot those scores when you're relaxed and flowing and there's no-one around to put you off in terms of crowds or TV crews."

Of course this is a tricky scenario to engineer as few golfers can afford to slip out of contention just to free themselves up to play! But the point is that knowing better golf is likely to flow when you're relaxed should encourage you to try and find ways of staying relaxed in situations that would normally make you nervous. Being able to distract yourself meaningfully away from the source of worry can take all shapes and forms – perhaps humming a tune to yourself, learning how to control your breathing when the pressure is on, talking to your caddy or playing partners, or simply taking more note of your surroundings. Anything really that stops you dwelling on your inner thoughts and concerns, and helps you switch your focus to the external environment.

Experiment to see if you can find a tension release strategy that really works for you.

Turning points

The 1990 Open at St Andrews was a significant turning point in Jamie's career, boosting his confidence and self-belief. Little surprise that in the following week's Dutch Open he recorded a career-best – at the time – 6th place. That final round in Switzerland had a significant turning point early on too. Jamie remembers: "On the 4th hole I hit a terrible drive down the right and I was right behind the trees and a water hydrant. The only shot I had was with a driver and my caddy looked at me like I was mad. I cut the ball about 40 yards in the air, got it on the green to 20 feet and made par, and just kept on making birdies after that. It was a one-in-five shot that came off and early on I think that was a turning point."

Many rounds have turning points one way or the other. If you can latch on to the positive ones – risky shots that come off, lucky breaks, long putts to save par when bogey looks certain – then it's possible to gain positive momentum for the following holes or even the rest of the round. However a round is going, momentum is only ever potentially just one shot away.

Going for your shots

Jamie observed that Ronan Rafferty went for his shots in that 1990 European Masters and feels this is a trait all top players share: "When you look at all the boys on TV who are playing well – Singh and Woods – they go for everything. They really do. They allow their talent to come out." The value of a high-tariff shot that comes off can be colossal in terms of confidence, but these shots become more viable with a bit of specific practice. Jamie knows how valuable that kind of practice can be: "We go on the range and muck around and practise hitting 3-woods and drivers high and low. I'm quite inventive and normally do take things on. I tend to think 'there's a gap there.' I'm a bit like an 18-handicapper when it comes to things like that. I want to have a go at it, and normally I do."

But there's one crucial difference – the average 18-handicapper convinces himself he can pull off miracle shots he really has no idea how to execute; Jamie goes for them knowing he can play them. Annika Sorenstam famously applies a '6 out of 10' golden rule to any potentially risky shot. If she thinks she can execute it successfully six times out of 10 she'll go for it; otherwise she'll leave it for the practice ground. And if even a top professional works on a 60% success ratio, it's probably wise for us to increase that further in line with our ability, and the repertoire of creative shots we have in our lockers. So it perhaps becomes an '8 out of 10' rule for us.

Ultimately, if you do decide to go for it, you need to be able to stand there and say, "I know it looks a bit risky but I have played this shot before and think it's worth a go." That's fine as long as you're prepared to accept the downside if it doesn't come off. You made a choice, and decided it was worth the risk. Fine. Forget about it and focus on the next shot – no regrets, live with your decision. And if it does come off? You'll give yourself a huge boost and potential momentum builder. It all comes down to belief really – belief that you've been doing the right things in practice and not merely doing things right. You could have been practising wonderfully well, but unless that practice has included elements to specifically help you play these 'go for it' shots, it will be of no use to you when it comes to the crunch.

Assuming the belief is justifiably there, once you've decided to 'go for it' you mustn't allow any internal gremlins to creep in and sow seeds of doubt as to whether or not it's the right thing to do. If there's a little voice nagging away in the background saying, "I hope this will be okay", "maybe this is silly" or "I know I don't normally do this so it is a risk" you're unlikely to make a normal swing, but rather a quicker one, a slower one or one where your head's up looking for the ball before you've even made contact… and we all know what the most likely outcome then is. Only go for these shots if you've made a 100% commitment to the decision.

A gradual dawning

As Jamie bagged birdie after birdie that Sunday afternoon, he resisted the temptation to simply play with reckless abandon. By the time he reached the 10th tee, he realised there was no point in throwing away the good work he'd done so far by being foolishly aggressive, so decided to be sensible for a while and wait for better opportunities to attack: "I got to the 10th tee and I thought 'calm down a bit', because 10 to 13 can catch you out a bit round there. There are a couple of blind shots, and the 11th is a long par-3. So I said to myself, 'just calm down a bit. Don't be silly, make a few pars here, and then we'll have a go at the finish.' You could always have a go at the finish round there in those days."

So even in a round where Jamie knew he needed as many birdies as possible, he was still able to exercise prudent caution and bide his time. This is a good lesson for any golfer – don't try and force things on holes that are reluctant to have anything forced out of them. A good strategy is absolutely vital, and you need to be very clear in your mind as to when it's best to attack, and when it's best just to play par golf. Holes that command respect should be approached with just that. Better opportunities probably await.

As it happens, Jamie birdied one of those respect-commanding holes, and when a fleeting glimpse of a leader board showed that Montgomerie had bogeyed the first, certain thoughts first entered his head: "I thought, 'hang about, I'm not too far behind here.' I got to the 14th tee and said to my caddy, half-joking and half-serious, 'if we can go eagle, birdie, birdie, birdie, birdie, we can win this.' And although it was a joke, I knew I could do it because it was potentially on for anybody in the field."

Those comments made half in jest were sufficient to trigger a mental reaction in Jamie: "That was the first time I started to become nervous. For the first time it kicked in that I had a chance here, because I knew that I was playing well." The simplest thing now would have been to let nerves take over and immediately wipe out any possibility of victory. But Jamie didn't – he wasn't about to back off now.

I can do it

Over the next couple of holes things progressed from a vague realisation that something special might be on, to real belief. When the early part of that final five-hole plan came to fruition, rather than scaring Jamie into backing off or becoming over-defensive, it actually enhanced his self-belief, so that when the 30-footer for eagle went in on the 15th he really felt, "right, now I can win."

He didn't allow his mind to start focusing on the outcome and tell him he couldn't really expect to play the last five holes in six-under. He became totally focused, stayed firmly in the present and simply did what needed to be done: "I knew on the 16th tee what I needed to do, and that was all I thought about. I thought, 'three holes here, if I can birdie all three, that's it. Let's do that and then worry about it afterwards.' When I look back, I'm proud of the fact that I knew I could win. I still had three holes to play but I went off and did it. I didn't get to the next tee and back off."

Jamie set out to take care of everything he could take care of, then leave the rest up to the others. That's all you can do – look after yourself. But if you do that well, it can have an impact on others. Jamie knew that if he could achieve what he wanted to over those last three holes, that might be the case: "I thought, 'well if I can get a score in, I don't care who they are, it's going to make them think.' From having a five-shot lead to suddenly being three behind is a kick in the whatevers for anybody."

If you simply attend to your own business on the course and do it well, it can have all sorts of beneficial implications – especially if others are unable to do it as effectively as you.

Staying in control

Arriving at a short par-4 16th tee wanting three birdies, you might well be tempted to reach for the driver and have a pop. Jamie didn't, but this wasn't a decision borne out of doubt or fear. He weighed it up and decided that as his short irons were so good that day, the best way to make birdie was via a wedge approach: "I got to the next tee and my caddy wanted me to hit driver because you can drive the 16th – but it's very narrow. So I decided I would hit 5-iron off the tee because I knew I was wedging it really well and I thought, 'no, I'm going to keep my game under control.' And I hit the 5-iron, wedged to about 10 feet and holed that. And that was a great feeling because I knew how in control of my game I was."

So an apparently cautious approach was actually a positive play in Jamie's mind. Eagle wasn't his target for that hole, and he knew he was playing well enough to have a great chance of making birdie the conventional way without risking the tight drive. In fact, Jamie felt it was in some ways a courageous play, as the expectation for someone in his position might have been to go for it. Whenever you make a similar decision on the course, you must ensure that when you hit the shot, you have eliminated the voice of doubt. You have to be clear in your own mind that you're definitely doing the right thing before you address the ball. In that way it becomes a positive play to you, regardless of what others may think.

Starting low, going lower

Unbelievably low rounds don't happen straightaway for most tour pros. Besides needing a swing and game physically up to the task, there are mental barriers to overcome as you take yourself into new territory. Jamie has shot in the low 60s a number of times, but remembers that starting low, and then going lower was another learning curve: "When they get to three- or four-under a lot of guys back off and end up shooting 69 when really they could have shot 66. They're quite happy getting to three- or four-under but when they get to five- or six-under they feel anxious and start thinking, 'Oh my God – I'm going to shoot 65'. And you ask yourself, 'well, why didn't I shoot 65?' And I remember Ray Floyd saying that when he gets in that situation all he thinks about is making another birdie. Then if he makes another birdie he just wants to make another one. That's the way to get over that." All you should ever be trying to do on the golf course is to play the next hole as best as you can.

Jamie has crossed that difficult hurdle sufficiently well to no longer feel unduly frightened when the red numbers keep racking up: "You learn to get over that. You have to learn to say 'well, if I want to shoot 62, I've got to learn to be comfortable and just keep playing the shots.' There comes a point in a round where you've just got to say, 'I'm after a birdie on this hole.' Forget where you are – if you're eight-under or whatever – 'I'm going to make a birdie on this hole.' You've got to take yourself away from the round situation, which is a great trick to learn and to have."

The key to going really low is simply the age-old adage – 'one shot at a time'. Forget about what's gone before – all you're ever really doing on the golf course is playing another hole. If you can get into that frame of mind then it doesn't matter whether you're seven-over or seven-under at the time. Easier said than done, certainly, but the reality is that whatever's just happened, the only thing you've got to do next is play another hole. So stick to your routine and don't allow yourself to be pulled this way and that by the health, or otherwise, of your scorecard, or the events going on all around you.

It's not over yet

Even when Jamie had achieved his three-birdie finish and the incredible round was over, he still had his feet firmly on the ground, even though some were encouraging him to crack open the champagne prematurely. He'd started three hours before the leaders, and there was still a lot of golf to be played.

So although the press were virtually handing him the trophy, he knew it wasn't all over: "When I came in I think I was five clear, and I did my press interview and they were all saying 'oh you've won it now.' But I never believed I'd won it, which was a great thing I'd learned previously to that. I said to myself, 'If I can do that, I know Colin Montgomerie and Anders Forsbrand at the peak of their games can do that.' So I knew it wasn't over."

This wasn't defeatism by any means, but rather realism borne out of past experience. Jamie knew that if there were to be a play-off, it would be hard to lift himself for it if he'd already mentally awarded himself the trophy. So when Anders Forsbrand rattled off five closing birdies to tie, Jamie was able to cope: "I never once allowed myself to think I'd won it which was a good thing as I don't think I could have handled the disappointment of it all. Because I felt things had gone against me a little bit in other tournaments where I thought I was going to win and didn't, I didn't allow myself to think I'd won until it really was all over."

Staying positive

When Forsbrand was inconsiderate enough to birdie the last five holes, Jamie's level-headed approach had left him suitably prepared for the play-off. He certainly wasn't thinking, 'here we go again, another one gets away?' Far from it: "No, I wasn't thinking that at all. There was a little pitching area between the 18th and the 17th. I knew the play-off was going to start on the 17th so I went down there with my caddy immediately after Anders had holed his putt and for five or seven minutes just hit some 60-70 yard pitches to get myself back into my game." No fatalistic, negative thoughts. Just a matter-of-fact 'let's get ready for the next phase.'

Things looked bleak on the first play-off hole when Forsbrand virtually drove the par-4 17th, and Jamie's second shot got no closer than 25 feet. But when Forsbrand either thinned or overhit his approach and had to get up and down to stay alive, the momentum perhaps changed. Jamie then decided to adopt a very positive approach to the second play-off hole. "Well, I'd dodged the bullet really. If that was the bullet, I thought, 'right,'- because I was a bit tentative on the first hole – 'stop pissing around. Let's make birdie.' And I hit 3-wood up the middle. We were both up the middle and we both hit similar shots in to around 15 feet. And I'd decided I was going to birdie it whatever he did and ran mine in." Moments later, Forsbrand's putt stayed above ground and Jamie was the champion. He had retained his positive frame of mind in the play-off, and achieved what he had set out to do on that final hole.

Future benefits

It was a great feeling for Jamie to win in such unlikely circumstances, and one that helped him going forwards too. He had made the transition from believing he was good enough to win, to actually proving it: "I knew then that I could see off a tournament which was good for me. I knew that given the chance again I could use that experience and go on and do it again."

For a variety of reasons, that didn't happen for another seven years. A bout of the shingles disrupted things the following year and there were more near misses too. But the moment finally came in the 1999 Moroccan Open, in a relatively weak field which again helped Jamie as he knew that his experiences of contending and actually winning would stand him in good stead coming down the stretch. Again the course was set up to Jamie's liking and he was playing well – positives that he drew on to produce a winning final round of 64: "Yes, I did say to myself: 'You've got to have a go at it here. You've got to go for your shots.' There were a lot of inexperienced players on the leader board and I knew that they would be backing off – not all of them – but I knew that they would be backing off. I thought, 'if I can get a run going here, I'm not going to back off. Today I'm not going to back off. I'm going to keep going for my shots.' In fact I think I was three or four clear going down 15, and had a 3-wood in over water and was still going to go for it. It was only when my caddy said 'you're four shots clear' that I thought, 'alright, I'd better lay up!'"

In Switzerland, Jamie had been confident, relaxed, and in control enough not to panic when it dawned on him that there was a real chance of winning. And although the second win took a while to come, when it did he was able to draw on some of those Swiss experiences to see him through. None of this is to say that winning is ever easy, but rather that being in a certain frame of mind on the course can make it more possible. As for the future, Jamie would love to notch up win number three: "For sure the second one's harder to win than the first. I'm sure the third one's really hard as well, but I'd like to find out." And if he does get the chance to contend for that third title, he may well be able to draw on the experiences of the first two to carry him home.

Preparing for Fame

Fame More

Fame More, one of Britain's brightest young female golfing prospects, realised from a young age that her golf could become more than just a pastime. After a successful amateur career that included two Curtis Cup appearances, Fame joined the professional ranks at the end of 2004 and set about trying to fulfil her dream of playing golf for a living in the belief that her experiences as an amateur had prepared her well for her golfing future.

"When I played my first Curtis Cup I only played one game and lost it, and that can upset the apple cart. But I think you've got to come away and draw the positives from it. Then in two years' time you can be in another similar situation and approach it very differently. Your outlook changes. But I do think that only comes from both good experiences and bad experiences really."

Many golf clubs are blessed with strong junior sections, but only a small minority of those juniors will be female. And although plenty of girls may at least give the sport a try – particularly if their parents are active members of a golf club – there is a greater tendency for them to drop out during the senior school years than the boys, as other things come along to distract them and take priority. Fame More is one of the exceptions. She was introduced to the game by her father at around 11 years of age and within quite a short space of time had become pretty good at it. She was the Golf Foundation's 1996 champion in her age group, and the same organisation's Golfer of the Year in 1997. She became the England schoolgirls' champion in 1998, and captained the England schoolgirls' team for three years before making her full England debut in 2000 at just 19 years of age.

A host of other honours followed including a place in GB&I's Vagliano Trophy team in 2001, where she caught everyone's attention by winning all four of her matches. She represented GB&I in the Curtis Cup in both 2002 and 2004, and won the English Mid-Amateur at Moor Park towards the end of 2004. Many things have gone well for her. Others, like those two Curtis Cup experiences, not so well. But nothing swayed her from making a decision in late 2004 that she'd probably first started pondering back in those highly successful junior days – to become a professional golfer.

The transition from amateur to professional is a brave move for any young golfer, but it requires an even greater leap of faith for women, as the opportunities for them to make a living playing the game are more limited than for their male counterparts. They have fewer tournaments to play in, lower prize funds to compete for, and no mini-tours – certainly in this country – on which to learn their trade. Their amateur careers have to wholly serve as their apprenticeships.

So Fame's decision to turn pro was perhaps borne out of an even greater determination and desire to follow her dreams than it might typically be for a young man of a similar age. We take a look here at some of the issues and decisions Fame faced as her golf progressed to the stage where she felt that turning pro was the right move to make.

You can't do it all

Talented golfers are often quite good sporting all-rounders, and golf was not the only sport that Fame was good at during her school years. In the men's game, Nick Faldo was pretty handy on a bike, Mark Roe excellent off a diving board, and Freddie Jacobson a dab hand with the table-tennis bat. Fame was a pretty good all-rounder too playing tennis, hockey and netball to a sufficiently high standard to be considered for county trials in the latter two. But when Fame's golf progressed rapidly enough for her to make the England Girls U-18 squad when she was just 14, it dawned on her – even at that tender age – that if she was serious about her golf, something else would have to give. Looking back, Fame says: "It was getting to the stage where I obviously had to make a decision because I just couldn't do them all. I decided to give my golf a go because it was something that I really wanted to pursue, while tennis and the others were more recreational things. Golf was too to start with, but when I was about 16 I was starting to think that this was what I really wanted to do seriously."

School years are the ones where kids can enjoy a more broad-brush learning experience than later life usually affords, so specialising at such a young age involves considerable sacrifice. Once Fame decided she wanted to give golf a real go, it wasn't just other sports that had to take a back seat, but also her higher education. Fame explains: "I did go to university but I was only there a year and took a leave of absence because at that time, in 2000, I was in the GB&I squad. It was a gamble I took because I thought at that time I could always go back to my education, but I couldn't go back to my golf. There were so many people always calling round on me at uni, and I thought if I did get into that way of life, my golf would suffer. And I wasn't willing to do that."

Fortunately Fame's family and friends understood and supported that decision taken in her teenage years, which must have been a huge relief to her at a time of life when the expectations of parents and others can weigh heavily on young shoulders. Looking back, Fame feels that narrowing her sporting focus at school and abandoning her university course were sacrifices worth making, because she could already see that if golf were to be her long-term future, then they were really her only options – much as she missed the social side of team sports and university: "You certainly sacrifice a lot of your time to practise and play but if you want to do it, then you have to. You can't do everything, can you? It comes down to choices you make at the time and what seems right really."

Choices surrounding your golf will probably not be as life-encompassing as the ones Fame had to make, but if you do reach a stage where you want to take your golf up a level – whatever that level may be – you will almost certainly find that you can't do it unless you re-arrange your life sufficiently to afford golf greater focus and time. As Fame realised, you just can't do it all.

Pressure and criticism

Top level golf, particularly at times of breakthrough, involves learning to cope with a number of different things such as self-generated pressure to perform, the expectations of others, criticism that you sometimes perceive as unfair, and failure to achieve what either you or others think you should be achieving. As Fame progressed into the national set-up, she felt that the pressure to perform increased considerably. Some of this came from within, but some also came from outside sources, giving Fame a kind of unspoken 'we've picked you, now we expect you to deliver' feeling. That was certainly the case when she burst through into the England first squad. Fame describes it in this way: "There is always pressure put on you I think, but then once you've actually been in it for a couple of years you do realise that there are expectations placed on you too – not intentionally I don't think. But people obviously do expect you to perform."

In 2001, when Fame was picked for GB&I's Vagliano Trophy team against Continental Europe at just 19 years of age, she promptly went out and won all four of her matches, instantly raising the standard she would subsequently have to live up to. More pressure, and certainly more expectation, as Fame continues: "You're suddenly placed in the limelight and as soon as you don't quite perform – perhaps they expect you to win or whatever – people can be very quick to criticise. But that's just sport, isn't it? I don't think there's any specific way you can deal with it and it can very easily get to you."

After missing the cut in the British Amateur in 2002, Fame felt her subsequent selection for the Curtis Cup set some tongues wagging, but that those tongues belonged to people with short or selective memories. That in itself made things worse, because failure to perform then would in some way have vindicated those who felt she should never have been selected in the first place. Fame felt that pressure very keenly: "There was obviously a lot of pressure on then. I did get picked because of my past record, and people were very quick to say I shouldn't have been because they had already forgotten what I had just done six months ago. It does bother you and I'd be lying if I said it didn't."

The British press and critics in general, are of course notorious for having short-term memories. One bad result seems to block out all recollection of previous successes. You're only as good as your last result is a frequently expressed sentiment, yet one that is hopelessly inaccurate and extremely unhelpful – certainly in golf. What about all the results that went before – were they just flukes? Nick Faldo cited his treatment at the hands of the press as one of the main reasons for his full-time departure to America in the late 1990s.

Fame, of course, has not yet reached that level of national repute. But words can cut just as deep in a regional newsletter or from an important figure's mouth if they're less than complimentary about you, and in your mind, unfairly so. The key to dealing with this is to examine yourself honestly, establish whether any of the criticism is justified, and then take action to deal with it either way. If it is justified, address and resolve the issues. If it isn't, then it may be better to just put your head down, and get on with things the way you want to. This is the kind of self-preservation option that has caused some players to break relations with the press temporarily or permanently during their careers.

For Fame, some of the criticism she endured was perhaps instrumental in her decision to turn pro as she realised there are fewer people you have to keep happy in the pro ranks – ultimately only really one: "I just thought 'this is rubbish. I've just got to do this for myself. I don't ultimately want to be an amateur golfer.' I think then you've got to start looking at the bigger picture and realising what you really do want, and I think at that point you end up taking the pressure off yourself. You're still working just as hard but you're doing it for yourself and not for what anyone else thinks about you. It's what you think that counts, isn't it, rather than someone else's opinion? Why should they criticise you if you come 2nd in the British Strokeplay for example, when even if you came last you could still be quite happy?"

Re-evaluating success and failure

It's all about honest self-appraisal really. Even if on the face of it you haven't performed in the eyes of others, you can still be satisfied if you've tried your hardest but things just haven't worked out. Listening to, and focusing on, unjustified or uninvited criticism can definitely hamper your progress. Being comfortable with yourself whatever the outcome will leave you in a more positive frame of mind going forwards. Golfers are only human, and if you've genuinely tried your hardest there's nothing wrong with saying 'well, it wasn't really the result I wanted, but I did this or that well, and a couple of things just didn't quite work out. But I never stopped trying and I'm happy with my game really'.

It's important to be clear about the distinction between outcome and performance goals. Most people unfortunately lean heavily towards the former, in which money, wins, top 10s, low scores or perhaps a handicap cut would constitute success, while missed cuts, poor finishes, high scores and handicap increases would be regarded as failure. Far better to set yourself performance goals that are more to do with how you approach your golf than what you score, as they'll provide scope for success every time you play. If your goals ask you to stick to your game plan, give 100%, and not to give up on your score, and you can answer yes, yes, no to them in your post-round self analysis, you will have succeeded regardless of the figures on the scorecard. Tiger Woods says his father never used to ask him his score, but rather inquired as to whether he'd given 100% and what he had learnt. The outcome was of secondary importance. Similarly, Johnny Miller remembers his father simply asking, 'what did you learn and what did you enjoy?'

I'm only human

Blocking out criticism becomes harder the better you get and there is a growing temptation to listen to anyone and everyone in your desire to improve. The wider the interest you attract, the louder the critical voices are likely to become, and in moments of self-doubt it must be hard to shut them out. But if it's unfounded then that's exactly what you must try and do. Fame has found this hard at times, but has tried to remind herself that she's only human – even if others forget that – which automatically brings with it a degree of fallibility.

By readily accepting her humanness, Fame has become better able to cope with those who question her when she doesn't actually win. Fame sums it up this way: "It's very hard sometimes to put it to one side because you always feel that people are watching you. But you're not going to go out there and perform week-in, week-out. That's sport in general. But people forget that. They just think that you're a machine or that you've done it once so you can do it every time."

It's important to be aware that in golf, or any sport, harbouring thoughts that every single practice session or tournament must be an improvement on the previous one is an unrealistic expectation. Even the very best golfers such as Tiger and Vijay in their respective all-conquering years, will have lost more times than they won – albeit only just in their cases! Most people would regard Ian Poulter as a successful golfer. He's won over 8 million euros on the European Tour, finished top 10 on the Order of Merit three times and at the time of writing was one of the top 30 players in the world. But if you look only at his win record, he has lifted seven European Tour titles out of 200 or so attempts, representing a strike rate of just 3.5%. If you regard anything other than victory as failure, then you're going to fail an awful lot of the time in golf, more so than in most sports. So thinking of it in those terms must be counterproductive for virtually every golfer.

Finding positives in failure

Failure and success are such stark terms that it can be hard for others to see that one performance might have elements of both in it, even if you yourself are able to view it that way. Your personal goals for any given event may differ considerably from the expectations of others, and if that's the case it's important that you subsequently evaluate your performance relative to your goals rather than theirs. An inability to take anything positive out of an apparent failure can set you off down a very dangerous mental path, so Fame has learned not to see every so-called failure as something terminal, preferring to always try and find a positive slant whatever the result seems to suggest. This is not always easy but it is always beneficial, even if it's simply a matter of saying, 'I think it didn't come off because I didn't do that well enough, so I really need to go away and work on that for next time.' Be honest by all means, but don't descend into a doom-and-gloom mentality – that's really not going to help. It might be a good idea at the end of a round, tournament or season to actually write down what was in your control and helpful and then what was not in your control and helpful. Then do the same for what was in your control and unhelpful and what was not in your control and unhelpful. Once you've done both, you will have a clearer picture of the controllable things that you should focus your energies on, and the uncontrollable ones that are not worth wasting precious time over.

Fame chooses to try and leave the worst bits of any bad experiences in the past, while taking what she can from them for the future as she explains here: "I think you've certainly got to draw a line under them, but I think you've also got to come away and draw the positives from them. From any bad situation I think you can always draw some positives. At the time it might be terrible and you might think that it's the worst week of your life and you're never going to quite get over it. But you always do, and there is always a positive at the end of it. If you can't draw some positives from it then I think there's something wrong really."

In late 2004, Fame headed off to America to try and qualify for the lucrative LPGA Tour, but was unsuccessful in that particular venture despite coming very close to making it through. Rather than wallowing in her disappointment, Fame has chosen to bank it away as useful experience for the future: "You can't be too negative. Yes, it was disappointing but I've still got some positives from it. You'd never go out and do it again if you were that negative on yourself all the time, would you? I mean you can get really down in the dumps and think 'that's it; I'm useless' and compare yourself to everyone else. But if you can walk away from a week and think you've given it 100%, then no-one can criticise that even if you've not been successful, can they?"

For you too it would be wise to try and find at least something positive in every round – even if it's only one or two shots. Focusing on them will be far better for your mental golfing health than wandering round with a figurative 'end of my golf is nigh' board draped over your shoulders. Tiger Woods has said you can either mope or dust yourself down and get on with it. Which do you think is going to be better for your golf? Sometimes this is known as the ALF technique – Accept what has happened; Learn from it; Focus on the things that matter to you.

Doing it for yourself

Fame has found the transition from amateur to professional golf a liberating experience in some ways. In team golf there are always others to think about – team-mates, captains, selectors. In professional golf, the only person you really have to worry about is you, and whether you're meeting the goals and targets you've set for yourself. Fame remembers that change of focus: "I got to the point where I was just doing it for myself. I wasn't doing it for anyone else. I said to myself, 'it's for me that I want to do this, I haven't got any points to prove to anyone really.'"

Fame also believes that taking greater charge of her own destiny has made her a stronger character, and one better prepared for her future as a professional golfer: "It's made me become more decisive and I actually know what I want to achieve for myself. Everything really in an amateur season revolves around some sort of team selection, and you structure your year around those things and think it's the be-all-and-end-all to get in those things – which it is. But ultimately if you want to be a professional golfer then it's more than that. You should really be thinking about individual performance more then anything."

Turning pro is a defining moment when your thinking has to change from 'am I good enough to make it?' to 'I am good enough to give it a go.' It can be liberating in that it brings an end to the internal 'should I, shouldn't I?' debate and re-clarifies your focus. It was like that for Fame as she goes on to explain: "I think things like that just do make you a stronger character and actually you realise what you want from your golf. It's really secured the fact that I do want to – well obviously I have now turned professional – but I do want to be a successful pro."

Follow the dream

Turning pro is not the culmination of Fame's ultimate golfing dream, but an essential step along the way. And she hasn't allowed setbacks to throw her off the scent – although there have been times of doubt. Looking back to 2002, Fame recalls: "I missed the cut at the British Amateur and then didn't have a particularly great Curtis Cup, and I did sit down at the end of that year and ask myself if this was really for me. I really had to re-address how I went about things because if I was ever going to give it up I potentially might have considered it then."

But she didn't, and the result of that self-questioning session was that it made her more eager than ever to see this thing through to whatever its ultimate conclusion may be.

Having a plan

Ambition is great as long as it's accompanied by a well-thought out, step-by-step master plan that embraces short-term, mid-term and long-term goals. Rather than focusing only on a distant goal it's far better to look at where you'd like to ultimately be, work out the steps you'll need to take to get you there, then focus on one that is within reach in your desired timescale. Then if you achieve that, you're a step closer to your ultimate goal. That first step could be a mental thing, like determining not to let bad breaks get to you as much, or a physical one such as realising your chipping is costing you several shots a round and needs some attention. When you've resolved that satisfactorily, move on to the next mini-goal. This must be a better approach than focusing on something that's so far in the future – or perhaps even physically beyond you – that the path to reach it becomes demoralisingly daunting.

Realistic goals

Fame certainly feels that a realistic approach can be a positive rather than a negative one: "I think you've certainly got to be realistic. I'm a very self-critical person and I know at times that can be a disadvantage, but I do think it can also be an advantage because there's no point in being unrealistic. Whether you're a top amateur or whether you play club golf, there is no point in setting your sights too high. You've got to actually realise what you can accomplish and what you need to do to accomplish those things."

There must be countless players on tour who know deep-down that they're never going to be Tiger – or perhaps even a top 10 or top 50 player – but who are quite capable of playing well enough each year to earn a very nice living from the game. All the ambition and work in the world will probably never take them to the very top, so would it not be better to work hard at retaining what they've got rather than beating themselves up mentally to achieve something that will always be beyond their grasp? That may sound defeatist, but what is really worse for your mental state – striving for the unachievable, or knowing your limits then striving to achieve right up to them? We think the latter really has more positive overtones to it. And of course, things change all the time that allow you to modify your plans, so it's a good idea not to make your goals so rigidly watertight that there's no room for movement. Sometimes it can be difficult to see beyond current form, and as any golfer will tell you, form can fluctuate so dramatically that when you're at a low ebb it's easy to lose sight of your real potential. At that particular moment it seems way beyond your reach, even though deep down you know you've reached certain heights before and are therefore physically and mentally capable of reaching them again. So goal-setting always needs to be a careful blend of ambition and realism.

Failure to achieve highly specific outcome goals is likely to occur on a regular basis, so if you only think in those terms it becomes harder and harder to view any other result in a positive light. Fame is certainly aware of this potential pitfall: "I do think that you've got to set goals and I think that those goals can probably change as well. But I don't think you can be too specific with your goals in terms of 'I want to win X, Y and Z' because at the end of the day it might not – probably won't – happen, and I don't think you should then be critical with yourself if it doesn't."

Fame knows what she wants – to be a successful professional golfer. And she's already taken many steps to make that more of a possibility – narrowing her focus as a schoolgirl from many sports down to just one, giving up a university place to follow her dream, not being afraid to go her own way, taking positives out of apparent failure and setting goals for the future that are achievable rather than overly fanciful.

Her long-term goal when she first turned pro was to be a successful player on the lucrative LPGA Tour in America, and as we've already seen, her initial attempt to secure a place there via the annual tour qualifying school proved unsuccessful. In 2005 she decided to return to the UK to try and establish herself on to the Ladies' European Tour, making it through the qualifying school for her home tour at the first attempt towards the end of that year. She then went on to make eight out of 16 cuts in her first full year on tour in 2006, with a season's best of 10th place in the Swiss Open helping her to successfully retain her full playing privileges for the 2007 season.

As Fame settles into life as a touring professional it will be interesting to see how well her experiences in the amateur ranks have equipped her for a golfing world in which every shot played has a monetary value attached. One thing's for sure – if she does eventually make it to the very top, she certainly won't need to change her name!

Bear pit necessities

Colin Montgomerie

When Colin Montgomerie stepped onto the 1st tee on Ryder Cup Sunday in 1999 it wasn't just reigning US Open champion Payne Stewart he found himself up against, but also a hostile crowd – a minority element of which proved willing to stop at virtually nothing in its efforts to distract him from the task in hand. This is the story of how he coped when things turned decidedly ugly that Sunday afternoon in Brookline, Massachusetts.

"I was there for the team and I was doing a team's job. I backed off the putt because of the team; I holed the putt because of the team; I walked from the 6th green to the 7th tee and said what I said loudly for the team's sake. Everything was for the team."

We've all endured good-natured barracking from our regular golfing partners as we try to hole that crucial five-footer to close out the match and leave them footing the drinks bill. Some of us may even have played in important matches away from home where we've been only too aware of any spectator allegiance. But very few of us have had to endure anything like what Colin Montgomerie faced during the infamous 1999 Ryder Cup in America. If we were to, just how would we cope? Would we wilt like under-watered flowers in the midday sun, or use adversity to strengthen our immediate resolve and determination, before storing it away in the memory bank to use to our advantage again another golfing day?

This chapter is not a blow-by-blow account of Colin's Ryder Cup week at Brookline, but rather an insight into what went on inside his mind throughout that notorious encounter, and how he was able to turn apparent negatives into positives to strengthen his game, rather than letting the unsavoury events destroy it.

Biggest name; biggest threat

But how had it reached the stage where one of the most civilised of all sports could degenerate into an atmosphere that Sir Michael Bonallack, and later Mark James, likened to a bear pit? As far as Colin is concerned, the roots can be traced back to the 1997 US Open at Congressional when he cracked and answered back to a heckler: "From then on I was never going to be number one in America. I was also the biggest threat – I was for many years in the US Open and Ryder Cup. I was the biggest European threat and that plagued me and followed me through '97 and '98 and of course through to the 1999 Ryder Cup. I was the best player and therefore also public enemy number one."

It should also be remembered that after two successive defeats, America simply couldn't afford to lose a third consecutive Ryder Cup – especially on home soil in front of an expectant crowd. This was brought home in an alarming way to Colin when he inadvertently walked into the opponents' locker room on the opening day to be confronted by a huge 10 foot by two foot banner proclaiming, "losing is worse than death; you have to live with losing." In Colin's mind, the reason for everything that happened to him that week was that he constituted the biggest obstacle to what America desperately needed to achieve, and therefore to a certain element of the crowd he simply became fair game with no holds barred.

Comfortable in the leading role

Quite apart from being fair game in some American spectators' eyes, Colin was clearly the European team's figurehead both in his own mind and that of captain Mark James. Colin recalls: "I was given seat number one on Concorde next to the captain. I was given priority everything. I was Mark James' number one player, and anything I said or did went. That's how I felt, and I felt that way the whole week. Mark had said that, the team knew that, and that was it. Olazábal was experienced, but I was the one who was going to – not make or break that Ryder Cup – but put it this way, if I played badly we weren't going to win."

This elevated role sat very comfortably on Colin's shoulders – and with good reason too after ruling the European Tour with a rod of iron for seven years and developing into a highly accomplished Ryder Cup matchplay exponent. Mark James' affirmation of his standing within the team simply served to further boost his self-belief – a useful weapon to go into action with, especially for the type of battle in which he was to become embroiled that week.

He also used other means to further bolster his self-belief in the face of extreme adversity throughout that testing week, even down to selecting his own playing partner. The original plan had been to pair him with fellow Scot, Andrew Coltart, in the foursomes. But he gelled better in practice with another Scot, Paul Lawrie, who had plucked The Open Championship out of nowhere just two months earlier to force his way into the team. They got on well, their caddies got on well, and Colin also gained some satisfaction from the fact that the reigning Open champion was looking to him for guidance and advice. So come the final fourballs, when the ever-present Scottish pair faced Tiger Woods and Steve Pate in a match that effectively became Colin and Tiger head to head, he was very much up to the challenge, and confident enough not to allow the mighty Tiger to bulldoze him aside.

Trouble brewing

Back on day one, although there had been a few hints of what was to follow in terms of crowd 'participation', their opening foursomes match against David Duval and Phil Mickelson passed off fairly uneventfully and successfully for the

Scottish pair. But Colin did notice a very different interpretation of the 'team' concept between the two sides. While the Scots walked together, Duval and Mickelson walked 50 yards apart. You can read what you want into that, but Colin chose to use it mentally to his advantage. In his mind, Europe played as a team; America didn't. Whether that was actually true or not didn't really matter. What did matter was that Colin used the 'team' notion as his main source of inspiration throughout the entire week. So even if the reality were different to his perception, it still had a beneficial effect in the one place that really counted – Colin's mind.

As the contest progressed towards Sunday with Europe amassing a 10-6 lead on Saturday night – a margin that was beyond their wildest dreams – Colin was only too aware that the atmosphere was taking a turn for the worse. On paper an American team boasting a big world ranking superiority should have simply brushed Europe aside. Yet Europe's young underdogs now stood on the brink of a remarkable success. And because the US team wasn't delivering the goods out on the course, Colin began to detect "a huge America against Europe. American players; American marshals; American spectators; American viewers."

This mood had been growing throughout the second day when Colin and Paul had faced Hal Sutton and Jeff Maggert in the morning foursomes. The first significant 'incident' occurred on the 6th green where Paul had hit a nice tee shot to around six feet below the hole. As Colin took his putter back to attempt the straightforward right to left uphill putt, an American voice in the crowd rang out as clear as a bell, "miss the putt". Colin backed off, went through his preparation again, and with grim determination slotted the ball firmly into the centre of the cup. As he left the green, he recalls, "I then saluted – not to the hole, nor to the putt, but to this idiot in the crowd." As he walked to the next tee, he said loudly to Paul, within earshot of Sutton and Maggert, "they don't understand what that's doing to me. That just makes me so pissed off and so motivated and so ambitious to win that it's actually backfiring on them altogether."

He was convinced that Sutton and Maggert had been quite accepting of the crowd's performance so far – a kind of tacit approval – and that his comments would later find their way back to the US team room. He imagined a hypothetical report-back along these lines: "Monty is the leader of this team. He cannot let the team down and if he doesn't perform, we know that we're going to beat this team. He is performing – we're in trouble, right. And if he performs, everyone else gets a bit of a lift. They're a very young team and they're being lifted here. This is bad. We need to do something with the crowd here. This isn't working." Whether this was actually being said or not behind closed doors we'll probably never know, but the antics of some American players on Sunday afternoon certainly appear to bear this out.

Doing it for the team

Before jumping ahead to the disgraceful final day incident that Colin had to contend with, just what was it that enabled him to not only cope with what was being thrown at him, but almost even to thrive on it? Much has been made of the way European Ryder Cup teams seem to be able to bond together as a unit more readily than US teams. It's not really for us to speculate here as to whether American teams really don't gel, but rather to look at the extreme importance Colin placed on the whole concept of 'the team', using it as his primary motivating force to help him through what were undoubtedly the most unpleasant on-course experiences of his career.

Time and again Colin confirms that "doing it for the team" dictated all his responses to the personal verbal aggression he suffered – in much the same way that novice London Marathoners might choose to focus on the deserving cause set to benefit from their fund-raising efforts to help block out or overcome the pain barrier. Colin reminded himself repeatedly that he was doing this for the team, not himself: "I was there for the team. My personal record in the Ryder Cup means bugger all to me. Okay, people say 'you've won 23.5 points'. Big deal! I'm there for a team and I was doing a team's job."

So how did this help? It meant that he was able to mentally divert any verbal attacks away from himself and onto the team. They were only being directed at him because of his extreme value to the team he was representing. This made it not only perhaps slightly more bearable – though far from desirable – but also created a worthwhile reason for withstanding it. By deflecting the venomous insults away from himself, he was able to de-personalise the abuse as much as humanly possible, and use it to fire himself up rather than allow it to grind him down. In a perverse way the insults were actually compliments – the crowd wouldn't be having a pop at him if they didn't think he was good enough to represent the biggest obstacle to US victory.

That's all well and good as a kind of altruistic theory, but how did he actually shut out the distractions in practice, particularly at the critical moments of shot execution? The answer is that he conjured up an image of exactly what he wanted to be doing on Sunday night. Colin remembers: "I had to focus on something, and what I wanted to do was to hold the Ryder Cup on Sunday night and fly home. I think you need something to keep you going. There needs to be a purpose to all this barracking. If there weren't a purpose you'd just walk in. You'd think, 'this is pathetic.' I don't need to be here. But I couldn't walk in. It was the Ryder Cup. So you got on with it."

The thought that he was doing everything for the team, and was able to imagine himself holding the trophy on Sunday night, spurred him on to keep going, rather than throwing in the towel. This became all the more crucial in the worst incident of them all on the 9th tee during his singles match against Payne Stewart on Sunday – more of which in a moment. Golf isn't played in a noise vacuum – there's always a buzz or hum in the crowd, and always the chance that another player on a nearby hole will provoke a big crowd response just at the top of your backswing. That is part and parcel of the game to which players become conditioned. What they are not conditioned to is the kind of targeted verbal attack Colin endured that Sunday afternoon – a lone voice hurling obscenities purely because of the flag he represented and the threat he posed to American domination.

You just have to deal with it

In singles matchplay, every golfer is an island. If he succeeds, it's down to him. If he screws up, it's down to him. So if the crowd turns on him in a singles match he doesn't have the instant support system of a partner to turn to – he has to deal with it himself and either sink or swim. What happened to Colin on the final day in his singles was far worse than anything that had happened up till then, but he still believes that choosing to focus on the much-hoped for team result helped him get through it.

Things had turned unpleasant not long into Colin's singles match, with Payne Stewart helping to get an abusive American fan evicted as early as the 4th hole. Colin describes the atmosphere with this analogy: "It got to that stupid stage where it was ridiculous, so bad – you know it was like when your child says something so bad that it's almost unpunishable. That was how it was. It was so bad and so poor that it was bizarre."

Things really came to a head on the 9th tee. After Stewart had driven, Colin stood up, addressed the ball and prepared to play. As he reached the top of his backswing a lone American voice cried out, "miss it you c**t, you European c**t! Go home!" The very worst of language in the most gentlemanly of sports. This single remark so upset Colin's father that he was no longer able to cope and returned to the clubhouse in shocked disbelief that such things could happen in the professional golf arena. But it did happen, and Colin had to deal with it – on his own this time as Stewart had just got back into the game and had his own corner to fight.

Colin turned to the crowd to remonstrate with them, warning them that if anyone else shouted out they'd go the same way as the previous evictee, before eventually regrouping enough to drive off with his legs still shaking.

It shouldn't happen in golf; it has no place in golf; but Colin had to cope with it regardless. How? Again it was back to the team scenario, and the belief that if he cracked, Europe would find it harder to win – an outcome that was still distinctly possible at that stage of the afternoon. No-one should have to go through this kind of thing, but if it does happen, you have to find a way to cope or you're beaten – regardless of whether or not it's fair. Colin wasn't scared as such, but this incident took him way out of his comfort zone into an area where a professional golfer just shouldn't have to go in the normal course of duty.

Turning negatives into positives

His response to all these incidents was to find ways of turning negatives into positives, leading to a growth in determination rather than a cracking of resolve – an own goal from an American perspective. Colin recalls how he was able to approach shots in the face of this heckling by first being prepared for it, and then being desperately keen to disappoint those whose sole intentions were to put him off his game: "It's like everything. If you expect it to happen, you're prepared for it – and I was. Paul Lawrie wasn't and had to prepare himself for every incident. Every shot I hit happened to be sort of booed and cheered and what have you, and I was getting to the stage of expecting it, and almost – not enjoying it – but enjoying hitting good shots when the expectation was of something else. I loved that."

That's far from saying it ever reached a point where Colin would have chosen to play under those conditions. But by accepting it and realising there was little he could do to prevent it from happening, he simply had to come up with an alternative coping strategy if he was to remain effective. One of these strategies was clearly his desire to do his best for the team, and another was getting added personal satisfaction from being able to lift his game and produce the very opposite quality of shot to that which the crowd was hoping for – the art of turning apparent negatives into performance positives, with a kind of 'right, I'll show you' attitude. To a certain extent Colin feels he almost revelled in the situation: "Looking back I really enjoyed Brookline, you know. People say how the hell could you? But you know I did; I really enjoyed the pressure and the challenge of that type of environment."

In hindsight, could – or should – the European team have developed an advance strategy to help them cope better with what they faced? Colin had to some extent, because of the heckling he'd already experienced in America on previous visits. But beyond that, how could there really have been a team strategy to cope with this onslaught? No-one could have foreseen the depths to which golf crowd behaviour would plummet that week. So strategy really had to be made up as they went along, with every man coping as best as he could in his own way.

Part of Colin's approach was to adopt a positive rather than negative approach to worst case scenarios. That's not to say he lowered his expectations on every shot, but rather that if things didn't quite pan out as he would have hoped, well… life still goes on; the next shot still has to be played. But his mind was only ever focused on the shot in hand immediately before and during the critical stages of execution thanks to a solid pre-shot routine designed to help him cope with any kind of distraction. Colin simplifies it in this way: "It's just a golf shot after all. You should be able to shut out whatever's happening. And I managed to do that over the ball. When I'm taking strike of the ball there's nothing that I'm thinking about but visualising the shot, and making the club and ball emulate what I've seen in the air. That's it."

Putting it all into perspective

He also developed a philosophical way of aiding concentration by dismissing the potentially worst outcome as having no lasting consequence in the overall scheme of things. Whether you feel from having watched him over the years that he has always followed his own advice here doesn't really matter – he believes it. If someone who makes his living from the game is able to think this way, how much easier should it be for us, for whom the game is but a pleasurable distraction from the daily grind? Colin's next comment is one we should all bear in mind whatever level of golf we're currently playing at or aspiring to: "It is the classic case of 'what's the worst that can happen to this shot or putt?' You can miss it. If that's the worst that can happen, then what's the problem? You put it into that context – using a double-negative if you like – so that two wrongs do make a right, or can make a plus if you want them to. If that's the worst that can happen, well that's all right. I can cope with that and get on with it – and that makes it easier."

Colin also felt in his own mind that he was able to rise well to the challenge of the next shot immediately after a poor one, or an outburst of some kind – much like tennis's 1980s superbrat, John McEnroe, whom Colin felt always managed to lift himself for the next point after one of his regular temper tantrums or disagreements with the umpire. So when he had to hit that tee shot with his legs shaking on the 9th tee, he had mentally regrouped sufficiently to be able to do so, drawing on the knowledge that he had produced the goods in difficult circumstances at other times in his career. Colin explains: "Yes, very rarely do I let it affect me for the very next shot. It's amazing how good the next shot is. You do tend to relax. It does tend to calm you down somehow with an outburst like that. It can work both ways. It can finish you, or if you are a strong character as I am, it can work in your favour." You have to know yourself, know your emotions, and know which ones you need to keep in check. Whether this all fits in with your opinion of how Colin seems to react when things aren't going his way is irrelevant. If he feels he has the mindset to bounce back after adversity, he is one up mentally on the golfer who allows any kind of disaster to precipitate a huge slide. What's done is done. You can only influence what happens next.

Turning up the concentration

We've talked about the need to shut out distractions, but that's easy to say and perhaps harder to actually do. So exactly how do you achieve that when you're used to playing in front of polite, courteous crowds and are suddenly confronted by a rowdy mob? This isn't football, where the fans believe an entitlement to vent their fury is included in the ticket price. This is professional golf, and this sort of thing has not traditionally happened. The problem of how to cope can also be exacerbated by the simple fact of not knowing when you're going to need to. As Colin recounts: "You weren't quite sure when it was going to happen and how it was going to happen. There were different situations involved, and you had to cope with them as they came. Eventually I just tried to shut it out for the sake of my partner. I couldn't let him down"

But shutting out an unknown quantity is no easy thing. For Colin, a famously quick player, the answer was to start taking longer over shots – almost providing an opportunity for it to happen. He also talked more to his partner than he would normally do, and fell back heavily on the experiences gained during four previous Ryder Cups. Even if nothing as unsavoury as this had ever happened before, the biennial transatlantic clash had always provided the ultimate pressure-cooker golfing atmosphere. Colin describes it in this way: "It's who can actually tee the ball up from the ground, never mind who's playing well. The pressure is intense." So he was able to switch into maximum concentration mode because he knew it was the only way to cope with the pressure, regardless of whether or not the crowd turned on him. It was a case of adopting golf's essential mental skills: "Yes you concentrate on that classic 'one shot at a time', and the classic 'don't get ahead of yourself'. I couldn't afford to because I was being barracked on most shots. It was an effort, but I did it. I focused in – really focused in on the shots. That's why I took longer I think, because I really concentrated on everything I was doing."

Concentrating on the shots is all well and good, but in the golfing environment they actually account for a very small percentage of a round. During the other non-shot phases, most players try to switch off before switching back on again when it counts, as it's simply not possible, or indeed necessary, to concentrate intensely for four or five hours.

Some players won't look at scoreboards during this downtime, as they don't want to let them affect the way they play their next shot. But this doesn't always work – most notably for Jesper Parnevik at the 1994 Open at Turnberry, where he refused to check the scoreboards, and came to the last hole mistakenly believing he needed a birdie. He attacked the flag unnecessarily, missed the green, didn't get up and down and walked off with the bogey that ultimately meant it was Nick Price who held the Claret Jug aloft. Colin isn't like that. He wants to know what's going on at all times – partly because it fills his time and mind with something other than potentially harmful thoughts between shots: "I enjoy every tournament, the way tournaments pan out and how they're won or lost. That's just me. Some people don't look at scoreboards because they're focused on their own game. Yes, I'm focused over the shot, but I have to have some sort of 'out' by looking at a scoreboard or finding out what's happening on other holes. Then, when you do come to the shot, you are very much switched on, and you can concentrate for those 15 minutes or so that you have to. But you cannot concentrate for five or six hours to that degree."

The school of hard knocks

We've learnt about the mental coping strategies Colin employed to prevent himself giving in to intense adversity that difficult week. But have these distinctly unpalatable events had a permanent detrimental effect on him? Far from it, according to the man himself: "Oh God, no, it hasn't left me scarred. It's made me much, much tougher to cope with. If I can cope with that 9th tee on Sunday in the Ryder Cup at Brookline, I can cope with anything in my job. That was the worst incident, I think, in the Ryder Cup and certainly one of my worst incidents... and I coped with it. I hit my shot off the next tee."

The toughest people are able to draw strength from adversity rather than letting it drag them down. Far from inflicting any lasting damage on him, Colin feels the 1999 Ryder Cup has actually left him a stronger person mentally, at least where it most counts for him professionally – on the golf course. With the unprecedented levels of crowd hostility he endured that week, it would perhaps have been perfectly understandable if he'd walked away and turned his back on America. And although he has on occasion promised to severely limit his US schedule, he has of course continued to play there.

He also went on to produce one of the most memorable Ryder Cup performances ever in the very next match at The Belfry in 2002, winning four and a half points out of five, perhaps using his Brookline experiences as a strong motivational force. And the Ryder Cup has continued to bring out the best in Colin, with the five further points he notched up in the 2004 and 2006 events taking him above Seve into 3rd place on the all-time European points lists with 23.5. Only Nick Faldo and Bernhard Langer have now won more, and their totals of 25 and 24 respectively are very much within range should Colin successfully make the team for a ninth time in 2008. If he does, he will probably still be the player many Americans dread most in the draw, especially in the singles where he remains unbeaten in eight attempts.

On top of all the positives Colin drew on to help him cope with the very worst kind of crowd hostility at Brookline, he also believes he subsequently benefited from a significant upturn in respect from both the press and some golf fans, who haven't always warmed to his occasional flare-ups in the heat of battle or just after an unsuccessful round. So overall Colin feels he took away a hatful of positives from what could easily have been a very damaging experience.

Go for it!

Colin's closing quote in relation to his experiences at the 1999 Ryder Cup could be just what you need to have echoing round your mind next time you tee it up in a potentially tricky environment: "If I'm scared of the crowd [or whatever], I shouldn't be here in the first place… But if I do this, this is fantastic! Come on; let's go for it. What's the worst that can happen? Stuff that, let's just go for it. As always, that's easier to say than to actually do. But that was a very different week. If you can cope with that in our game, you can cope with anything."

Great Scott

Scott Drummond

Rookie tour pros are supposed to go through what Scott Drummond endured in early 2004 – eight missed cuts from 11 starts and a best finish of tied 16th. What they're not supposed to do is then go out and win the prestigious PGA Championship on the back of that unlikely run of form. Incredibly, Scott Drummond did just that in May that year, shooting a final round 64 to hold the European Tour's finest at bay and catapult him from 435th to 95th in the world. Here's how he did it.

"I didn't get caught up in the fact that it was a flagship event or that there was a five year exemption and one of the biggest pay cheques on tour. I put all that aside and just stripped it back down to basics. I had belief in what I'd been working on, I had belief in myself, and I just went out there and played golf in its rawest form, which is hitting the ball, finding it and hitting it again."

Personality and lifestyle aside, there are many similarities between Scott Drummond's fairy-tale victory in the 2004 PGA Championship and John Daly's out-of-the-blue success in the 1991 USPGA Championship. Both started out on the reserve list for their respective events, both had no form to hint that a victorious outcome was even remotely likely and both have experienced very mixed bags of golfing fortune since their moments of glory.

For one week in May 2004, everything came together for Scott Drummond in an almost miraculous fashion. He was thrilled just to be teeing it up alongside the stars at Wentworth for a start – he'd been fourth reserve when entries closed and only secured his spot when Greg Owen withdrew through injury. Scott recounts his feelings when he learned he'd got in: "It was a big thing for me and I just really wanted to enjoy the week. I enjoyed the fact that I was there, that I had earned my place in the field if you like, and regardless of what I had done in the weeks before, I just erased all of that and felt I was starting again there that week."

What he had done in the weeks before was fairly typical of many players graduating from the Challenge Tour to the European Tour – golf's equivalent of promotion from Division 2 to Division 1 or perhaps these days, the Championship to the Premiership. The courses are set up a little tougher, there's more money at stake, and the very cream of the European Tour is competing for it most weeks. Scott was well aware that he was on a learning curve, so as yet had not become unduly concerned by the series of missed cuts he had endured, preferring instead to focus on the fact that he felt his game was coming together and likely to start bearing fruit soon, even if his results didn't back that up.

Results alone tend to portray things in a very black and white manner when really they're often in shades of grey that can change hue at any moment should another piece of the jigsaw slot into place. Scott felt that if the early part of the season had been spent getting the edges in place, then it wouldn't be too long now before more of the picture began to take shape: "Yes, I'd been missing cuts but I felt my game was almost there, not necessarily to win a tournament but certainly to get some top 20s and top 10s. I felt I was working on the right things. I just had to keep believing that I was working on the right things and that eventually it was going to click and I was going to get that one good result that would spur me on or turn my season around." Scott was choosing not to focus on results that a casual observer might interpret as yet another young pro struggling to bridge the gap from Challenge Tour to European Tour, but rather on the progress he felt he was making regardless.

Nick Faldo celebrates his remarkable win at the US Masters in 1996, and inset, with the famous Green Jacket.

Justin Rose on his way to victory in the 2007 Volvo Masters at Valderrama, and inset, in his earlier, more testing days on tour in 1998.

Zane Scotland deep in thought at the
1999 Open at just 16 years of age.

Kenneth Ferrie en route to his maiden tour victory in the 2003 Spanish Open.

Richard McEvoy: top of the class at the 2003 European Tour Final Qualifying School.

Jamie Spence: still the only European
Tour pro to shoot 12-under par 60 on
the final day to win.

Fame More is still working her way up
the ladies' professional ranks.

Colin Montgomerie tees off during his testing final day singles against Payne Stewart in the 1999 Ryder Cup, and inset, victory is sweet.

Scott Drummond defied all the odds to clinch the 2004 PGA Championship at Wentworth.

James Heath hopes the simple approach that served him so well during his amateur days will be equally effective in his professional career.

Gary Wolstenholme on his way
to 'Taming the Tiger' in the 1995
Walker Cup at Royal Porthcawl.

Matt Richardson: good enough to be World
Boys Champion in 2002 and number one
English amateur in 2004.

Greg Owen went from the depths of
despair to the heights of a maiden tour
success during a seven week spell in 2003

Dave Musgrove: the right words at the right time for boss, Sandy Lyle, in their 1988 Masters victory.

Pete Cowen gives invaluable
advice to Lee Westwood.

How many golfers do you know for whom the only thing that matters is the result? Results are important, especially when – as in Scott's case – they dictate how much you get paid at the end of the week. But they should never become the be-all-and-end-all. Shrewd golfers acknowledge there are times when they play well but, for whatever reason, nothing seems to happen or someone else just plays better. Rather than instantly pressing the panic button, that is the time to persevere, show some patience, believe in what you're doing and trust that the results will come. That's what Scott chose to do – have faith in the process, keep striving for improvement and simply let the results take care of themselves.

His 2004 record meant it was quite a surprise when a first-round 66 saw him comfortably inside the top 10. But with many of the big guns opening up strongly, and local favourite Ernie Els cruising to a 64, few took much notice – every rookie has the odd good day after all. However, as scoring proved tougher over the next couple of days, rounds of 71 and 68 proved good enough to not only keep him in the top 10, but actually see him teeing off in the final group on Sunday alongside big-hitting Argentinean, Angel Cabrera, who held a one-shot lead.

"Time for the rookie to wilt," crowed the critics inevitably ahead of Sunday's final round. But not this particular one, on this particular day. Scott was showing no sign of nerves despite Clarke, Els, Faldo, Goosen, Jiménez and others lurking menacingly. He reached the turn at three under par, still trailing Cabrera by one. But five more birdies coming home – taking full advantage of Wentworth's double par-5 finale – saw him finish two clear of the slightly bemused Argentinean who must surely have thought adding a closing 67 to a one-shot lead would be more than enough to see off any challenge, let alone that of a rookie whose career best was tied 16th a few months earlier. Cabrera's time would come the following year, but just how did Scott manage to compile that bogey-free final round 64 when all the odds seemed stacked against him?

Read on for an insight into exactly what was going on in Scott's mind that enabled him to pull off one of the European Tour's biggest ever shock victories, and become the first player since Arnold Palmer in 1975 to lift the prestigious PGA crown on his debut.

Not low expectations, but no expectations

The one good thing, if you like, about a run of poor form is that no-one – including you – has any reason to expect anything of you in terms of results. That's just how Scott approached the PGA that week. Yes, he felt his game was close, but there was nothing in the formbook to suggest he would even make the cut in one of the strongest fields of the year, let alone contend for the title: "My results had been really poor. I think if you've been on a good run of form coming into an event then maybe it would be more a case of expecting to do well, because you've had some good results and this is the one you really want to do well in. But for me, there were none of those feelings. I suppose rather than low expectations it was actually no expectations." No expectations about results, but still the belief that what he was working on was right.

There's a world of difference between low expectations and no expectations. The former has strong negative connotations – a kind of 'here we go again, things just aren't happening for me so I expect I'll miss the cut again this week.' The latter can act as a pressure release valve in that no-one expects you to do well so you're not overburdened with external pressure, and you aren't putting too much on yourself either because there's no reason to do so. Assuming you actually think you're playing okay but things just aren't happening for you – as Scott felt here – the latter allows you to take a more philosophical mental approach to each round. So you can say to yourself, 'my results might suggest I won't do much this week, but I actually think I'm playing okay so let's just go out and see what happens.' Surely it's better to approach things that way when confidence is not sky-high than to build up your hopes falsely, then end up walking off deflated and bemused at another poor showing in a big event when you'd unwisely convinced yourself that this was to be your day.

Distractions of the 'wanted' variety

Those who like to bet on golf and who follow the advice of top tipster, Keith Elliott, will know all about the so-called 'nappy factor'. Others will be left scratching their heads a little at the concept. So in simple terms, there is some statistical evidence to suggest that players who have recently become fathers often suddenly produce the goods on the course and are therefore worth a modest investment.

Why should this be? Well for professionals, golf almost has to be an all-consuming focus if they're to succeed, and yet when a child is born, something comes into their often insular and self-obsessed world that is actually far more important in the overall scheme of things – another totally dependent human being. That can give a real perspective jolt to even the most single-minded of individuals, and the knock-on effects can sometimes prove highly beneficial, though not always as swift as for Scott who was well aware that the arrival of daughter, Kiera, shortly before the PGA, had been a major life-changing experience: "We'd only had Kiera four weeks previously and I think that has a big calming effect on your life. I mean, the fact that everything's gone well with the birth and the baby's healthy is obviously a huge relief, and you're then just totally focused on that baby in those first few weeks and months."

Scott goes on to describe how his disrupted preparation for the PGA may actually have been a blessing in disguise: "I stayed in a Travel Lodge along the road and got an extra hour's sleep on the floor every morning in the duvet because my wife, Claire, was feeding. So in terms of what you might think would be ideal preparation, it wasn't at all. But in another way, it was, because it took my focus in the evenings away from thinking about where I was lying in the tournament, or 'what if I were to do this tomorrow?' Coming off the course to see Claire and Kiera, and having to deal with being a new dad, and both of us learning and all that kind of thing, really consumes you."

Life serves up many big moments that are so important and pressurised in their own way that they can sometimes generate a healthier overall perspective, even for the seasoned professional. Children are certainly one, but others such as marriage, an illness or death in the family or a new job can prove so all-consuming that to then approach your golf as a matter of life and death too would be too much for your mind to cope with. If even professional golfers can sometimes find themselves freed up to play by life's big events, how much easier should it be for those of us for whom golf is supposed to be but a pleasurable pursuit?

Ignoring leader boards

To look or not to look? That is the tricky question facing top players these days with regard to leader boards when they're in contention. The advantage of looking is that you then know exactly where you stand in the tournament and can respond appropriately to any challenges; the disadvantage of looking is also that you then know exactly where you stand in the tournament and might be drawn into either chasing the game or playing more conservatively in reaction to what the leader board has revealed, rather than sticking to your original game plan of simply playing one shot at a time, finishing the round, adding it all up and seeing if it's good enough.

There are perhaps sound arguments either way, but if it is your intention to stick rigidly to a game plan regardless of what's going on around you, then not looking is the only sure-fire way to avoid temptation. That way, apart from being able to see what your playing partner is doing, the only clues as to what's going on around you will be the volume of cheers ringing out – and even then you won't necessarily know why and for whom.

Scott wasn't normally one not to look, but then again, he'd never found himself in this situation before. So at the urging of his caddy, Kevin Smith, he decided to adopt this approach as soon as that first round 66 had sent him flying high on the leader board: "From the second day onwards I didn't look at any leader boards. Kevin said to me, 'if we're focusing on each shot in turn and forgetting about everything else then there's really no point in looking at a leader board.' I agreed that that was true, but at the same time it was very hard not to look, especially on the Sunday."

This may appear to be of slightly less relevance to club golfers, as the average golf club doesn't tend to have scoreboards scattered liberally around the course. But there can certainly be times when information is available to you that may dictate how you try and subsequently play. In a team matchplay event it can be all too easy for word to get back to you about how others are faring in matches ahead or behind, while the 9th hole often leads back close to the clubhouse or to a halfway hut where there's always someone who seems to know exactly how everyone else is doing and is only too happy to broadcast this information to all and sundry. And in a 36-hole event there will almost certainly be a scoreboard on display for you to pore over during the lunch break or overnight. So if you've decided that you don't want to be drawn away from your game plan under any circumstances, you must try and shut your eyes and ears to what you really don't want to see or hear, or at least try and perceive leader boards, or what your playing partners are doing, as 'information that is of general interest' rather than the trigger to deviate from your chosen strategy. Scott was somehow able to keep his leader board blinkers on in an arena where up-to-date information was all too readily available.

Just stick to the plan

With leader boards ruled out, Scott was able to play golf in it simplest form – hit the ball, find it, then hit it again. No chasing, no holding back and no changes to strategy in the light of events going on around him. Somehow, he managed to keep this up for the last three rounds: "We just didn't change anything from start to finish, which I think is a good thing because you can keep that equilibrium if you like. Yes, I knew I'd made some birdies and I must be somewhere up near the leaders, but going up the 18th on Sunday I didn't know the exact situation. I felt I was possibly tied for the lead. There was a huge leader board up on the right which I ignored, but just from the buzz of the crowd I knew I must have been up there. When Angel left his birdie putt short and I rolled mine in, somehow I just knew I'd won."

In fact, Scott stuck to the plan so successfully that when the BBC microphone was thrust under his nose by the 18th green he really had no idea exactly how low he'd gone that day. Scott sums up that little exchange: "Steve Rider came up to me and asked, 'How do you sum it up – shooting 64 in the last round to win?' and I think I said, 'I didn't even realise I'd shot 64,' because I was really not focusing on the score at all. I didn't feel I'd played my best ever round of golf technically, but obviously I had. It was one of the lowest rounds I'd ever had, but the ball wasn't always in the middle of the fairway or 10 feet from the flag. So that came as a big surprise."

We could all perhaps benefit from adopting a similar approach more often. But unfortunately many of us are guilty of being scorecard-obsessed, with our constant mental calculators telling us exactly how many over par we are, what that means in terms of our handicap or what we need to do to either keep things going or get them back on track. And the outcome all too often is the very opposite of what we're hoping for because we've allowed ourselves to get away from what good golf is really all about. Our golfing minds become filled with every thought other than the one we actually need to execute the next shot. They get clogged up with 'what ifs' or 'if I could just get to the turn without dropping any more' or 'I'm going to have to birdie all the par-5s on the back nine now', rather than simply giving each shot our 100% attention. Getting too far ahead of yourself usually guarantees that by the time you do get to where your mind has prematurely taken you, your score will no longer be worth bothering about!

'One shot at a time' says the caddy

Scott was fortunate to have Kevin Smith as his caddy. Not only did he do a good job, but he was also a sports science graduate with a good understanding of the mental side of the game. So Scott had someone close at hand to help him think straight throughout that big week. And after that string of missed cuts, Kevin was advocating something a little different. Scott recalls, "One of the key things for me that week was that Kevin had said, 'you've really just got to focus on playing one shot at a time. Don't think about a score; just give each shot 100%. Don't worry about where it finishes. Just get to the ball, focus on that next shot whether it's in the middle of the fairway, in the rough or whether you're chipping out of the trees – just get to the ball, focus on your next shot and don't think about anything that's gone before or anything that's likely to come up."'

Kevin had said this kind of thing before, but Scott recalls it was said with more passion that week perhaps because his caddy could also see that the way Scott was playing wasn't necessarily being reflected in his scores. For whatever reason, on this particular occasion, Scott was able to do just what Kevin was suggesting, and that week his thinking was spot-on: "Coming up the 18th or whatever hole, I wasn't thinking 'birdie for a 65' or 'par for a 67', I was just thinking about the next shot and then when I came off the course it was a question of 'okay, what score have I shot today?' People have said 'you looked so calm and collected all the way round' … it felt very surreal, but I was in my zone and my focus was fantastic. My ability, especially on that final day, just to focus on the next shot and not think ahead to all the glory and the tour exemptions and things like that for winning is something I'm proud of – that I was able to maintain that focus. Kevin was a big help there out on the course."

If Scott was able to maintain that focus with so much at stake, it perhaps shouldn't be too difficult for us to do likewise when the biggest things on the line are perhaps a fiver from our regular golfing mates and bragging rights for the ensuing week.

The right focus

In potentially pressure-filled environments, it can become easy to focus on the wrong things rather than the right things. Your head may be filled with thoughts of where you don't want your ball to go – that lake down the left or that deep greenside bunker – rather than where you do want it to go – the right half of the fairway or the safe side of the green taking that bunker out of play. Those who have played Wentworth's West course will know that many of the fairways are lined with trees on both sides, and that there is always somewhere you simply don't want to hit it. Scott knew all this but simply chose to shut it out and focus on the positives: "Everyone says that because it's so tree-lined and there are a lot of holes with out of bounds that you can run up some big numbers there on almost any of those holes on the back nine. But I just didn't feel it. I felt so confident in my game and in my swing, and I was so mentally strong that I could just picture where I wanted the ball to be and focus on that rather than the trouble that was all around."

That's not to say that you'll never hit the ball into trouble again. But thinking about what you want to avoid rather than where you do want to go can make it a more likely outcome, and also increase the need for stern self-recrimination – the kind you're likely to dish out to yourself after you've stood on the tee reminding yourself the jungle on the left is certain double-bogey country, only to find yourself moments later uttering the words, 'damn, not in there again' when your ball has come to rest... you guessed it, in the jungle on the left. The problem is the mind has severe trouble distinguishing negative commands from positive ones. If you don't believe us, try not to think of pink gorillas. The chances are that your mind is now full of vividly coloured primates even though your instructions were to not think of them. In the same way, if you think trouble on the golf course, then often that's exactly what you'll get.

Just enjoy it

This will either sound blatantly obvious to you, or perhaps come as a bit of shock depending on the state of your game right now or perhaps how long you've been playing. But golf really is supposed to be fun, and every single one of us will have started playing because we enjoyed it. For most of us golf is a pastime or hobby that takes up perhaps five or six hours of time in total for a full round and everything that goes with it. That's an awfully long time to spend doing something if you're not enjoying it, and while golf's frustrations can sometimes seem too much to bear, some of us spend far too long not enjoying it for it to make any sense for us to even be playing at all. Part of the problem is that most of us are highly skilled at logging our negative emotions and somewhat less proficient when it comes to the positive ones. So rather than allowing our positive emotions to build a wall of strength and confidence on which to rest our games, we tend to let the negative ones chip away at it until sooner or later it crumbles and falls.

We really need to keep things in perspective, and when it reaches the stage where fun would be the last word you'd use to describe your golfing experiences, maybe it's time to step away from the course for a while and either have a break or seek professional advice on how to get yourself out of your current rut. If the game can get to us that much, how much more might that be the case for those who play it for a living. Poor form equates to loss of income and added pressure to perform next time out, all of which can create an unhelpful vicious circle if allowed to go unchecked.

Thankfully, Scott chose to see beyond his current predicament of missed cuts and limited income and look ahead to the opportunities that lay before him in the belief that his game was almost there: "I decided to enjoy the tournament for what it was – for the venue, for the fact it was a well-run event and that there were big names playing. I wanted to enjoy it for that rather than letting that become a pressure in itself. I do want to win, but at the same time, I don't want to let that become a pressure that stops you enjoying what you're doing." A healthy perspective given the unfamiliar situation in which Scott found himself that week, but as he continues: "I was enjoying it – finally enjoying getting what I felt were some rewards for the work I'd been putting in."

Even so, there was still every reason to think that the final day would prove a 'rabbit in the headlights' moment in which he would freeze and simply be unable to perform. But along with everything we've looked at so far, there were other factors that Scott feels helped him through that apparently pressure-packed final day…

…a positive outlook

A run of missed cuts in lesser events was hardly reason to enter the tour's flagship event with any confidence or hopes of success, but Scott still chose to adopt a positive frame of mind to the whole situation. Rather than dreading it, he rationalised that the big money events over the next few weeks could be the ideal time to finally capitalise on the progress he felt he was making: "Funnily enough, I'd said to a lot of my friends that you only need two good results out of these eight tournaments coming up and you can pretty much have your card sown up for the following year. So I'd said that until those eight big money events were out the way, I wasn't going to start to panic as I knew, or at least felt, I was on the verge of some good results."

There are probably big events at your club that you have a secret or open hankering to do well in. But if you were approaching them with a run of results like Scott had endured prior to the PGA, would you find it that easy to be positive about your chances, even when relatively little is riding on it? Of course, if your poor run of form is down to some elementary problems with certain parts of your game then it's wise not to expect too much. But if everything seems pretty much in place – as Scott felt it was for him – then why should you approach that big event negatively if everything other than perhaps your results gives you no reason to do so? Yes, over-confidence or unrealistically high expectations can create problems of their own, but there is no point in burdening yourself with a negative outlook if the state of your golf simply doesn't warrant it. The best thing in these circumstances is to remind yourself that your ability is equal to that of other players, so you therefore have as good a chance as anybody else of performing well based on the way you know you've been practising.

... comfortable at the front

You'll often hear commentators say, "he may not have been in contention at this level before, but this guy knows how to win," before pointing to excellent records in the amateur game or on the lesser tours. Scott fitted that bill precisely, having enjoyed several successes on his way up to golf's top level. So come the Sunday of the 2004 PGA he was actively drawing on those previous experiences: "Whether it's on the UK mini tours or the Challenge Tour, whenever I've got myself into a good position in the tournament – whether it's in the top 10 or actually leading – very rarely have I had a bad last round or a bad weekend and fallen back down the field. I generally seem to thrive on being in contention and being up there. You know I do enjoy it."

What a great attitude to have! Of course it may not always pan out the way you want it to, but if there's evidence to suggest you do well when in contention why not let that override the nagging voice of self-doubt that's all too eager to have its say – even if you've moved up a level and are now competing on a bigger stage? The pressures, emotions and experiences of leading are fundamentally the same at whatever level. Yes, they become stronger or more intense the higher you climb, and many do indeed fail at the highest level. But surely it's better to tell yourself – as Scott did here – that you've experienced this before so know what to expect, rather than writing yourself off because deep down you think this may be a step too far. It's all about perception, so start off positively, see what happens and if you succeed, then great. If you don't, look at what went wrong, and how you need to approach it differently next time to reduce the chances of it happening again.

... last day pressure-busters

That final Sunday could so easily have become too much for Scott to deal with, but in addition to everything we've talked about so far, he'd already found a way to devalue the pressure that others might have perceived him to be under. As he looked forward to that final round, Scott recalls: "I knew that if I played a nice solid round of golf I would finish in the top 10, which for me would be a fantastic result and I'd be very, very pleased. Anywhere inside that top 10 would have gone a long way towards me keeping my card, which was my goal for the year. And a top five would actually have secured my card. That was a comforting thought, so I didn't feel that I had to go out there and win. People weren't expecting me to win, and I didn't put any undue pressure on myself to win."

At first you may view that as a slightly defeatist attitude, but you need to think of it in context. There was nothing on Scott's European Tour CV to suggest that a win was likely, and if you think hard enough you'll probably find many examples from your own golfing life where you have viewed a decent finish as a good result even if you didn't actually win. That attitude probably allowed Scott to play with far greater freedom on the big occasion than if he'd built up his expectations unrealistically, given his past record and standing within the game, and decided only an outright win would represent a successful outcome. There were three further things that Scott felt conspired to ease the final day pressure. First and foremost, that man Kevin the caddy came up with more inspired words at just the right time ahead of Sunday's round, and it was just what Scott needed to hear as he recalls: "Kevin said to me before we teed off on the Sunday, 'whatever happens today and whatever score you shoot, just remember that no-one can ever take away from you what you've achieved in these three days and the fact that you're about to tee off in the last group at Wentworth within a shot of the lead.' That was kind of a comforting thing to hear and I think it took a bit of the pressure off."

On top of that, Scott felt that the tee-times had worked in his favour too, because the big names of Clarke, Faldo, Els, Goosen and Björn had gone off in the preceding games and taken with them a fair chunk of the gallery, who were no doubt assuming those big guns had more chance of catching Cabrera than the unlikely trio of Darren Fichardt, Joakim Haeggman and Scott Drummond, who made up the last two matches along with the Argentinean. Scott found this a real help in the early part of the round when it can be hard to settle, especially at Wentworth where the long, tough par-4 1st and 3rd holes ask stern questions right from the off.

And then finally the draw had paired him with Angel Cabrera, a player whose prodigious length and power-hitting meant that there wasn't even the slightest temptation for Scott to try and match him as that would be futile. This left him free to play his own game and the course, rather than be drawn into a pointless head-to-head battle: "It was the first time I'd played with him and he's obviously a big powerful hitter. So I'd decided I wasn't going to pay any attention to him and how he plays the course because it was going to be very different to my approach. So that was good for me."

An obvious performance gulf in terms of ability or length off the tee is probably easier to deal with than a scenario in which players are closely matched. We've all played with people who are a similar standard to us and hit the ball similar distances, and it can be quite easy then to get drawn into playing them rather than the course even if we're not playing matchplay. Perhaps they're ripping it, while you're not quite timing it that day but otherwise playing okay. The temptation then is to start going after your drives to keep up with them, or allowing yourself to be swayed over club decisions into greens, rather than just playing the course as you find it with the golf game you happen to have on a given day. It doesn't matter if you have to hit a club or two more than them into the greens if you're still hitting those greens and putting well. Far better to play with what you've got than strive for the game or distances you wish you had or would normally expect – you'll almost certainly get into trouble if mental weakness goads you into playing beyond your physical and technical limits.

There's probably no better example of this than Zach Johnson's par-5 strategy in his 2007 Masters success. Not one of the longest hitters on tour, Zach vowed not to attack the par-5s unless he was in an absolutely ideal position. The result? He never actually went for any of the 16 par-5s he played in two, yet still racked up 11 birdies and no dropped shots. Those who adopted more aggressive strategies fared rather less well. That par-5 performance alone contributed greatly towards his eventual two-shot winning margin. As Zach admitted afterwards, "I had my limitations." But by allowing for those limitations – which were purely distance-based – Zach was able to shatter the myth that the way Augusta is now set up means only long hitters have any real chance.

Scott's pressure-busters came together perfectly for him in his big week too and his advice to you would be that however big an event you've got coming up, putting undue pressure on yourself to do well is unlikely to enhance your chances of success: "That week, I was as excited about playing in that tournament as a club golfer might be building himself up all year towards the Club Championship. It's the tournament they want to do well in, but at the same time I don't think you should put too much emphasis on it. My coach, Keith Williams, always says to me, 'your golf clubs and golf ball don't know which tournament you're playing in or whether you're putting for birdie or double-bogey.' So it's just another game of golf and you've really got to take away all those factors – or realise that there are factors there that can build pressure, and that you can put too much pressure on yourself by recognising those factors and making too big a deal out of them."

Storing it up for the future

Since that glorious day in May 2004 things have not always gone Scott's way. He finished 23rd on the Order of Merit that year, rounding off the season with a gratifying 7th place in the Volvo Masters, before a so-so 2005 which saw him finish the season in 74th place. 2006 was a poor year in which he had to call on his exemption from that PGA victory to retain his full playing rights, and 2007 has been much the same.

Who knows what the future ultimately holds for Scott. But however his career does develop over the coming years, the way he coped with the unfamiliar territory in which he found himself during the 2004 PGA will surely hold him in good stead if and when he does return to the business end of the European Tour's leader boards. That's certainly the way Scott sees it: "The achievement of not looking at leader boards and staying so focused is one thing that I've taken away from that week. Mentally, that was the strongest I have ever been. So I now know what I can achieve mentally as well as physically. That was a barrier to overcome, but it then registers in your mind just what is possible."

Whether Scott's current form proves temporary or permanent remains to be seen. But the experiences he gained that week, and especially on that final day, are still there somewhere inside waiting to be drawn on once more if and when he does turn things around.

Hard work, clear mind

James Heath

You may only just have begun to hear about James Heath. But after an excellent final amateur year in 2004, he joined the professional ranks in 2005 off an impressive handicap of +5, confident that a combination of solid groundwork and simple thinking would serve him as well there as it had done in his amateur days. This chapter looks at the key non-technical elements that have helped shape James as a golfer.

"People think there's a special kind of way you've got to think on the golf course. That's a little bit laughable because it's really a matter of just trying to clear your head, and just trying to get the ball in the hole in the fewest strokes possible. If you can make it that simple then that's all you need."

At any given time there are many talented amateurs eyeing up a future playing golf for money. There's probably a handful at your club right now, at the club down the road and at a great many other clubs too – and all look like really good players to the average handicapper.

That makes several hundred talented golfers who apparently possess more golfing skill in their little fingers than most do in their entire bodies. But there's a problem – average field sizes of around 150 or so on both the main European Tour and its subsidiary Challenge Tour mean the vast majority will never fulfil their playing ambitions. There just isn't room for them all. Players who breeze round their home courses in five- or six-under without breaking sweat often simply can't cut it when they get to tee it up with the big boys. Some don't have that extra something that separates the wheat from the chaff; others can't find a way to complement skill with an appropriately intelligent golfing brain. The latter underachieve partly, or wholly, because they never develop the right mind for golf.

But what happens when supreme talent is married to a clear, uncomplicated golfing mind? You end up with a player like 24-year-old James Heath who rose steadily through the ranks to become England's top amateur at times during 2004, before departing the amateur scene with every confidence that he could make a smooth transition into the professional ranks.

As a teenager, James was the kind of junior you find at countless clubs – 'living' there at holidays and weekends, and spending every spare waking moment practising, playing or challenging friends to chipping and putting competitions. But it quickly became more than that for James and there were summer days when he'd spend 12 or 13 hours practising or playing. Little surprise then that he was down to scratch by 16, lifting the England U-16 trophy before that particular birthday milestone.

What happened over the next couple of years may have helped shape the golfer he would later become, because for a while he drifted, finding himself distracted – not surprisingly given his age – by girls, and also hampered by injury. James recalls: "There was a summer when I was 16 or 17 and I had a girlfriend for about a year and a half. And it was like I wasn't really in control and wasn't practising hard enough. I had an injury in both my wrists too and couldn't practise and it was like 'where am I going?' I've come such a long way since then and I'm proud of myself for taking the right steps to becoming a better golfer."

That's not to say that girlfriends in themselves are a bad thing! It's just that for James, becoming a great golfer was the bigger dream, and having a girlfriend was drawing him away from what he really needed to focus on to progress at a critical stage of his golfing development.

So once the girlfriend situation had been dealt with and the wrist injuries had fully healed, golf became James's all-out focus once more and the trophies soon followed thick and fast – the Golf Illustrated Gold Vase in 2001, the Greek Amateur in 2002, and in his final amateur year the two that convinced him golf should be his career – the Lytham Trophy in record-breaking fashion, and the English Amateur Championship. Two of the jewels in amateur golf's crown.

By the time James kissed goodbye to his amateur status he was playing off +5 – a figure that only fully registers when it dawns on you that every time he teed it up he needed five birdies and no bogeys just to stand still. It goes without saying that only technically gifted golfers can ever reach such a standard. But for James, an ability to think clearly, efficiently and logically both in preparation and on the course has been equally important. With his help we've pinpointed six key factors which have played a part in his success. Some of them overlap. Sacrifices, for instance, not only require you to give up things that look pretty tempting, but also that you put in plenty of hard work. James says there really is no secret – but perhaps that in itself is the secret.

Making sacrifices

No golfer gets to the top without making sacrifices. For James one of them was the realisation that girlfriends and serious golf don't readily mix because they're often competing for the same time and attention, and there simply aren't enough hours in the day to fully devote yourself to both. He knew he needed to give everything to his golf to get to where he wanted to be, and chose to forego certain things while he sought to pursue his golfing ambitions. There would be plenty of time for girlfriends later.

And it wasn't just girlfriends that had to make way for golf either. Just before and around 2004's Lytham Trophy, James sacrificed something else in his quest to improve – a few hours' sleep. All the more impressive when you consider the magnetic pull the duvet has for many twenty-somethings! James remembers:

"In April I seriously woke up – I couldn't sleep – because I so badly wanted to make some really good progress on my putting. Just when the greens were starting to get good around Lytham time I couldn't sleep. So I got up at first light to work on my putting. I'm talking 5.15 in the morning here. And I saw some improvement straightaway. I gained three or four hours' practice on everybody else because I got up that early."

That last sentence implies a double benefit – the physical one of actually doing the practice, and the mental one of being able to stand on the tee knowing – or at least believing – he'd done something his fellow competitors almost certainly hadn't. That's the beauty of sacrifices – they put you in a strong position mentally where you're able to say to yourself, 'I've done everything I can and more. Now let's go and play.'

What you're able to sacrifice will of course depend on your circumstances. Families and jobs tend – not unreasonably – to demand lots of time. But you don't have to neglect your loved ones or get up at some unearthly hour to make a telling difference. It could just be an early night rather than a late session down the pub the evening before a round that means something to you. Or perhaps taking a day's holiday ahead of a 36-hole competition so you can practise a little more, or arrive less tired and more confident the next day. For James, the sacrifices had to be greater to really mean something. But even small sacrifices can give you a significant mental edge.

A hard day's work

Modern society is awash with people wanting to achieve something without being prepared to put in the necessary effort. A quick fix is more appealing to them than the idea of working really hard at something and then seeing that work pay off.

There are two problems with this. Quick fixes are nearly always only temporary, and there really is no substitute for hard work. Just knowing that you've put in the effort can give you a huge boost. James felt that his dawn raids on the putting green definitely helped him immediately afterwards, and on into the season beyond: "I did loads of work on my putting for about two or three weeks leading up to the Lytham Trophy in 2004, and obviously I played well there. I putted great, and continued to putt consistently well after that. I wouldn't say I putted the best I ever have, but my bad rounds became better than my bad rounds of a year or two before. And that's just because in the April of that year I really worked hard and was able to hit the ground running." Pros often say ongoing improvements once you've reached a certain level become more about making the bad rounds better than the good rounds lower. The 66s are still 66s, but the key is turning destructive 76s into just 72s or 73s. This art of damage limitation is often purely the result of hard work.

Nick Faldo is a great example of the hard work philosophy. On leaving school he applied himself to golf as if it were a normal day job, heading off to 'work' at the golf club, spending all day practising and playing, then heading home again after plenty of overtime. His 'wages' were the child benefit money his parents 'paid' him, and he did all this because he thought it the most logical way to take his golf to the level he wanted to reach. In a similar way, James's 12 to 13 hour days instilled in him the work ethic he would later need for success.

It's highly likely that you won't be able to commit to your golf to the same degree because of everything else going on in your life. But your game will benefit from any extra work you can put in over and above the norm. If your goal is to knock three or four shots off your handicap this year, you'll have to accept that it's pretty unlikely to happen unless you're able and willing to put more work into your game than you've previously done – within the constraints of your lifestyle.

A class apart

The benefit of knowing or believing you've done more than anyone else in terms of preparation can be potentially huge. James is admirably hesitant to talk about what he feels sets him apart from others, pointing out that he wouldn't always know what they have or haven't done to prepare for specific events.

But he is aware that preparation is not a 'one moment in time' thing – it's much more than that. As he travelled to 2004's Eisenhower Trophy – his last big amateur event – he reflected: "I can't really say, for instance, what has set me apart this week because I think preparation is longer than that. Preparation isn't the week before the event; preparation is your life really." It must be reassuring to feel that everything you've done in your golfing career forms the foundation for your next competition, rather than just two weeks' intensive preparation immediately before the event.

Equally James feels that specific things such as those early morning putting sessions have sometimes given him a mental head start on his rivals, even if others have thought him crazy. About that putting practice, he recalls: "I just got up, went down the club and started practising, and the greenkeepers were laughing at me because I was up at such a ridiculous hour. I wasn't trying to tell everyone, 'I'm up there before you.' I just wanted to practise at an hour when no-one else would be."

Don't waste it

The game is littered with players whose golf never became better in reality than in their minds. In most cases, raw talent can only take you so far, and if you want to go further you have to take appropriate steps to ensure you don't become another golfing casualty – someone who was nearly good enough.

There's a pressing need to keep complacency at bay in today's competitive world. Very few complacent golfers make it onto the tour – even fewer remain there. The best approach is to recognise the talent you've been given, do everything possible to make the most of what you've got, then work hard to retain it and to acquire what you're lacking. James is only too aware of this: "There are lots of talented kids. Fortunately I was born with a bit of talent so really it's up to me. But I don't want to be looking back in ten years' time saying, 'I wish I'd done that.' I'm absolutely determined for me not to say that, so I think that's probably what drives me to practise so hard." James' approach is very much one of 'if it's to be, it's up to me'. In other words, he has realised that if he is to ultimately make it to the top, it really is down to him and the effort and hard work he's prepared to put in, over and above all the valuable help and advice he'll no doubt get from various other parties along the way.

This straightforward, honest approach will surely stand James in good stead. While some fall all too easily into the trap of thinking they've got it forever, he's working hard to ensure he never becomes a 'whatever happened to him?' player. It's those, like James, who realise that having it now is no guarantee of always having it, that stand the best chance of holding onto it.

Keep it simple

So far we've looked at some of the groundwork that has given James such firm physical and mental golfing foundations. But how does his mind actually operate out on the course? Reassuringly for you, the answer is 'simply'. As we saw in this chapter's opening quote, James believes simple thoughts work best and that there's no room – or indeed need – to overcomplicate things: "It's really a matter of just trying to clear your head, and just trying to get the ball in the hole in the fewest strokes possible. If you can make it that simple then that's all you need."

But you probably don't play off +5, and aren't blessed with a gloriously repeatable swing. So how can you think of it in such simple terms when all too often the game seems anything but straightforward? The answer is that even if you're not blessed with James's natural ability, the more you're able to let your game work on autopilot, the freer you'll become to make the most of the ability that you do possess. Driving a car is a good comparison – a task you perform on autopilot 95% of the time. If you're driving down a narrow road looking only at the way ahead you're fine. It's only when you start to think, 'this is a bit narrow; I'd better keep a closer eye on that hedge,' that you find yourself veering into and away from the hedge more erratically. You've switched from automatic to conscious thinking for a task that no longer requires it.

James's thinking is very simple. Don't abandon something that fails you once, if that same thing has worked for you 99% of the time previously. That would represent an illogical response to what in all probability was just a simple human error in the execution. We're not perfect and never will be. As he puts it: "You may hit a bad shot or a bad putt and say, 'that routine's not working.' But that happens – you hit bad shots. You've just got to stick through it – just stick, stick, stick – and in the end it will be okay. I suppose that's why I just think to myself, 'if I work hard enough – which I can control – it will be okay in the end.' Just stick to your guns and everything will be okay – that's the kind of thinking I've got when I'm on the golf course. Stay patient and the birdies will come." The important thing to remember is that skill takes time to really embed itself and you'll only know it's fully embedded once you're able to produce it in the competition situation. Until then, as you go through the process of developing a particular skill, patience is very much a key requirement.

So James has chosen to adopt a very simple approach to his mistakes while those skills are still being developed – he just tells himself to, "suck it up and get on with it." This must be a huge advantage over those who panic at the first hint of anything untoward, rather than riding it out and waiting for the benefits of years of solid preparation to kick back in. They adopt a kneejerk response and end up heading off at a tangent in a desperate attempt to resolve things. Unfortunately those tangents are usually cul-de-sacs, whereas what you have always known and trusted is a temporarily blocked through-road that is actually passable with a bit of patience. James has seen the kneejerk response in others, but resolutely refuses to go there himself: "I see guys – who shall remain nameless – who every time I see them are trying a new driver, or trying a new swing. You don't need that; you just don't need that. It's not about quick fixes. It's about getting something and sticking to it through thick and thin, because in the end it's going to come through."

Next time a bad round interrupts a good spell, don't instantly assume 'that's it, I've lost it.' Rather, stick to what you've been doing and assume everything will be okay next time out. Only do something more about it if things continue to go badly, and then do it in conjunction with either a professional or a sports psychologist, depending on whether you feel the problem is technical or mental. And make sure that if it's the former you consult a qualified PGA professional, and if it's the latter, an accredited sports psychologist rather than some quick fix merchant promising you the world in return for a not-so-small fee.

Growing up

Maturing involves a transition from someone else taking primary responsibility for your development, to you committing to undertake that role yourself. There may even come a point where people around you are urging you to work harder, but you yourself are comfortable with where you're at and know that any additional work is unnecessary or could even be counterproductive. James feels he has now made that transition – he has developed an internal self-policing mechanism: "I know now that when I'm not practising [when I should be] I feel kind of guilty. That may be right or wrong but for me that's how I am. No one can change me or tell me, 'James, you shouldn't feel guilty about that,' because I do."

That's not to say gentle encouragement won't still be needed from time to time, but rather that James now knows when to work and when to rest. He's grateful though for appropriate kicks up the backside in the past: "A few years ago it was in one ear and out the other. It took some help – not shouting and saying 'you're not practising', but rather 'come on let's sort this out'. Now I feel I'm in a cool place where I can take advice off people if they're talking properly – take it in and realise 'yeah, maybe I do need to start practising harder.' But generally now that isn't the case because I know if I'm practising hard or not." And it's not just about how hard you practise. It's about the quality of that practice too. You can spend hours and hours beating balls into the distance with no real sense of purpose, but it will probably be of less value than, say, a practice session that seeks to more closely simulate real golfing situations both mentally and physically. James, for example, is a great believer in 'one ball practice' because one ball is all you ever get in a round of golf. It's pretty easy to stand there and hole the second putt after you've seen how the first one rolls, or knock the second chip stone dead when you've seen how the first ball reacts on landing. But there are no Mulligans in competitive golf – one chance is all you ever get, so why not devote part of your practice schedule to 'one ball golf' to give your game a more robust edge when it comes to the crunch?

Whatever the precise nature of any practice regime you undertake, you have to reach the point where you're doing something because you know you have to – and actually want to – in order to climb the next rung. As James sums it up: "You've got to realise it yourself. I'm sure all these young golfers have dads or brothers or mums saying to them, 'you've got to practise harder.' But unless you realise it yourself, you're really not going to go any further. You've got to want to be out there; you've got to want to go and practise. You don't want to be out there because someone's told you." Everyone probably knows that they need to do certain things to improve, but that on its own is not enough to make a difference. It's only when that need spurs a real desire that things can really start to happen.

This chapter has been a little different to many in this book in that it hasn't addressed a specific event or moment in James's golfing life. But we hope it has provided a valuable insight into the development of a promising young golfer. Apart from an initial dose of God-given talent, very little else is given to any golfer on a plate. It's up to them to put in the hours, make the sacrifices, grow in maturity, and ultimately really want it for themselves.

On the course we've seen how James adopts a straightforward mental approach – "work hard and keep things simple". The order of this sentence is important. Do the hard work first and it will prove a lot easier to keep things simple, because that vital groundwork will have formed a more stable base. Anyone serious about their golf – whatever their ability – would do well to emulate this young man as much as their lifestyle and circumstances permit. Don't complicate a tricky game any further with unnecessarily complex thinking. This approach empowered James to produce a record-breaking 18-under par performance to win the 2004 Lytham Trophy – better than Tom Lehman's or David Duval's Lytham Open-winning tallies. And his analysis of that week is quite matter-of-fact: "I was just playing my golf. I suppose it's a nice state to be in – just getting on with things one shot at a time. I had an average of about 66 that week, so it was just 66 bubbles of concentration a round." 'Bubbles of concentration' – what a great concept to hold on to.

The start to James's professional career has, like that of many other young players, been steady rather than sensational. But if you look closely at his results since turning pro you'll see that it all represents progress in the right direction for a young man still on a learning curve. He finished 23rd on the Challenge Tour in 2005 and 14th in 2006 to earn Category 11 status on the full European Tour for 2007. That 2006 season on the Challenge Tour saw him secure his first professional victory in spectacular style, shooting a final round 62 to surge through the field in the Ecco Tour Championship. And at the time of writing James was settling in nicely in his first full year on the main tour, notching up top 10s in Indonesia and China early in the season.

We think this young man has a very bright future ahead of him, and yet so much to teach us from what he has already achieved and the way he has set about doing it. He came to realise from an early age that on the golf course, all you can ever be fully in command of is what you're doing, not what anyone else is doing. If you do your best and someone else does better, so be it. As James says: "You can't control it. All you can really do is put your best stroke on the green, your best swing on the course and work as hard as you can." And it's a lot easier to feel in control of your own game if you've put in the hours. After all, hard work can prove very rewarding.

Taming the Tiger

Gary Wolstenholme

He may now be England's most capped amateur after making his 200th appearance for his country in May 2007, but Gary Wolstenholme MBE has never been a long hitter by any top player's standards. In fact, just the opposite. So when he came up against mighty-hitting Tiger Woods in the 1995 Walker Cup at Royal Porthcawl in Wales, he had to rely on strength of mind rather than power off the tee to help him pull off a seemingly unlikely victory. Here's the remarkable story of that match from Gary's perspective.

"Forget about the opponent. He has no bearing on the way I should be playing the golf course. He can't run across and shout at me, he can't hit me over the head, he can't kick my ball in a divot. There's nothing he can do that affects the way I play that golf course… unless I let him."

Hundreds of years BC a mighty Philistine was scaring the life out of the Israelite army as they squared up to each other across a valley in Judah. Understandably, none of the Israelites relished the prospect of going head-to-head with the 9ft Goliath who had been making mincemeat out of all-comers for years. A long stand-off ensued until one day a shepherd boy called David turned up with packed lunches for his brothers.

Shunning King Saul's kind but cumbersome offer of a decent set of armour, young David went out to meet the giant armed only with his sling, five small stones, and the knowledge of past successes against threatening predators. The Almighty as an ally must also have been useful. The rest, as they say, is history. A deadly accurate shot from his sling felled the giant in one blow –

the invincible had been vanquished and with new-found belief the Israelites went on to rout the Philistines and win the day for their King. Step forward a few thousand years to Sir Michael Bonallack announcing the pairings for the first day's play in the 1995 Walker Cup at Royal Porthcawl: "And the final singles will be between Tiger Woods and Gary Wolstenholme." No other announcements had elicited any real response, but now the crowd reacted with knowledgeable ooohhs and aaahhs. Why? Because they knew that in boxing terms this would most definitely have been viewed as a complete mismatch. As Gary himself later summed it up: "At first glance it was definitely David and Goliath revisited."

Tiger's extraordinary exploits as a professional since 1996 are legendary, but what had he done as an amateur prior to 1995 to strike fear into the hearts of opponents? What hadn't he done might be a better question! He had become the first player to win more than one US Junior Amateur title, notching up three in a row from 1991 to 1993, he had carried this invincibility on into the senior ranks winning the next two US Amateur Championships (a third would follow in 1996), he had made three out of five cuts in the Majors he had played, finishing low amateur at that year's Masters and he had even been voted Golf World's 'Man of the Year' in 1994. A golfing Goliath at the tender age of 19.

So was Gary Wolstenholme really a 'David'? Maybe in the context of this match, because although he had a good playing record, with the 1991 British Amateur and 1995 British Mid-Amateur Championships his highest accolades at that time, what the crowd was really responding to on that Friday evening were two diametrically opposed golf games. Gary was steady and straight, but distinctly short off the tee. Tiger carried an arsenal of 300+ yard missiles and miracle shots, and was renowned for overpowering both golf courses and opponents with awesome regularity.

This then is the story of how Gary was able to focus on his own game rather than Tiger's to level the apparently uneven playing field and pull off a memorable victory – one which helped send the GB&I team on its way to a first home success in the Walker Cup since 1971.

Preparing for battle

The confidence-building foundations for Gary's success were being laid long before the first tee shot had been struck. Far from being intimidated at the prospect of facing America's star player, Gary's initial reaction had been one of "excited anticipation". In the remaining 20 or so hours before that match, Gary did everything possible to eliminate the kind of negative thoughts to which others might have succumbed. By drawing on past experiences and seeking out the 'positives', Gary would eventually arrive on the 1st tee in a state of prepared readiness, rather than nervous panic.

His form had been very good coming into the event culminating in an excellent victory in the British Mid-Amateur Championship at Sunningdale just a few weeks earlier. By his own admission, this had left his confidence sky-high.

He had also judged shrewdly that a slightly quirky golf course in wet and windy conditions could be a great leveller, representing a sterner test than the manicured fairways of America's Country Clubs. A British links in good old British weather was something a top British amateur could handle. Most Americans would rather stay tucked up under the duvet!

Peter McEvoy, one of the leading figures in English amateur golf, had often used Gary in the anchor role for England, and although Clive Brown was the GB&I team captain at Porthcawl, it was Peter who filled Gary's mind with inspirational words immediately after the ceremony. Gary remembers Peter coming up to him and saying: 'If there were anyone in the team I would have wanted to play Tiger, it would have been you. You won't be intimidated if he's 100 yards past you – you're used to being 50 yards behind, so what's new?

Where others might try to match him, you will play your own game because you won't even try to compete on his terms. You will do your own thing.' What better way to further fuel someone's self-belief and confidence.

It was also effectively a 'no lose' situation for Gary since few others really believed his short-hitting game could finally topple Tiger from his invincible matchplay perch. Gary's view was that, "if you're going to lose, lose to the best player – not some lesser light, because there's little credibility in that." And to counter any 'defeatist cop-out' cries, Gary was clearly relishing his big-stage chance to silence the doubters in front of the TV cameras and large crowds: "Yes, if you lose, you've lost to the world's best amateur – but I wanted to win!"

But it was going to be tough because Royal Porthcawl certainly did not feature in Gary's top 10 favourite courses list, presenting him with several tough drives and a number of holes that would demand 5-wood approaches. Since he had not been selected for the morning foursomes, he would also be going in 'cold' in the afternoon. But to counter these 'negatives' Gary was aware that Tiger didn't appear to be particularly enjoying the Walker Cup experience, and would not be relishing Royal Porthcawl's challenge in the best of British links weather.

All of this was helping to steamroller the playing field in Gary's mind, and prevent him from being overwhelmed by Tiger's reputation and capabilities. A couple of days earlier, Tiger had reputedly reduced the par-5 17th to a driver, 9-iron albatross two in a practice round. But Gary refused to be caught up in this, insisting that, "if I play my way of playing, then I've just got to concentrate on that and not really worry about what he's doing at all. Pars and birdies win matches, not reputations."

Heading back to the hotel that Friday night, a combination of excitement about the match, and team-mate Gordon Sherry's Billy Connolly tapes had put the GB&I squad in high spirits. After reflecting on his match for a while, Gary consciously switched off for the evening, and allowed himself to be distracted by the Big Yin's unique brand of Scottish humour. Later on, a lively team dinner provided the perfect antidote to what tomorrow might hold. Saturday was the time for fine-tuning his mental and physical preparation. However big an event is, it's always a good idea to allow ample scope for downtime and relaxation to give yourself the chance to escape the intensity that often hangs in the air. Sometimes this will be arranged for you courtesy of 'official' dinners such as Gary enjoyed here, but at other times you may need to create your own relaxing diversions. They're as important as any practice regime in your overall preparation, so should be planned naturally into your schedule in just the same way. There's a time to work and a time to play – or perhaps in the golfing context, a time to play and a time to relax.

In the morning, he enjoyed a normal practice session under the watchful eye of his long-time swing mentor, Peter Thompson, then made his way back towards the clubhouse to work on his chipping and putting. Sticking to a normal routine creates a positive mindset; deviating from it can serve as a negative influence by suggesting something out of the ordinary may be lurking around the corner. For Gary, there is no substitute for solid preparation. He explains: "This is the key criterion as far as I'm concerned. Preparation is virtually everything, because if you're prepared for every eventuality, then the mental side becomes happier and more relaxed. And when I've done it all, then I'm ready to play."

With his tee time looming, Gary was drawing on other 'positives' for reassurance: he was an accomplished England player with many caps, he had played the anchor role in the past, he had coped with the ultimate pressure of the 1st tee at Augusta when playing The Masters as reigning British Amateur champion in 1992, he had played a few holes in the morning to get a feel for the course, he had good friend Colin Edwards on the bag and his mum was also there to 'share the experience of what he was going through.'

Gary was now looking to use any adrenaline to his advantage by channelling it towards the 'fight' rather than 'flight' response. His preparation had been perfect, he was ready to play and he just couldn't wait. Just like David as he faced the original Goliath all those years ago, Gary had not been tempted to change his own game to match his opponent's capabilities, preferring to focus on his own strengths and feed on past experiences for confidence. Any nervousness as he approached the tee was "not fear, but rather anticipation."

Doing battle

A formal handshake with Tiger suggested that conversation was not going to be a high priority for the young American, but Gary didn't mind, as he was now "in the zone and ready to play." The Almighty had also helped out by providing a wind that was against and off the left up the first. This would make the 2nd, 3rd and 15th holes tough, but Gary was more relieved that the 326-yard 1st was now out of Tiger's range and therefore a genuine par-4 for both players. So the David and Goliath battle commenced, and with Tiger now denied any possibility of a two-putt birdie on the first, the opening hole was halved in regulation fours.

The 477-yard par-4 second was a daunting prospect into the wind for Gary, calling for one of his best drives just to make the fairway. With Tiger's drive still some way distant, Gary's well-struck 5-wood approach finished just off the green to the right – mildly disappointing but considerably better than being the wrong side of the out of bounds fence down the left. As Gary walked forwards to where Tiger was assessing his approach, he was trying to turn his short driving into a 'positive'. Gary explains: "A tactic I often employ in matchplay is to perhaps intimidate my opponent by walking forwards. My ball's in play – he's then playing catch up, and that's sometimes the way I play in that scenario."

Whether it had any effect on this occasion is unclear, but moments later Tiger's misjudged 6-iron soared out of bounds through the back of the green and on to the beach. When his second ball also missed the green, Gary's solid chip was enough for a concession. First blood to the Englishman. Not only had he coped with one of the toughest holes – he had actually won it. The effect on Gary's confidence so early in the round was significant: "At that stage, in my mind, there was no way I wasn't going to be able to compete with Tiger in those circumstances on a course I knew well."

And it was a case of déjà-vu on the downwind par-5 5th, when Tiger again surrendered his 100-yard advantage off the tee by hitting through the green with no more than an 8-iron. Gary vividly remembers seeing Tiger's ball strike a bald spectator standing on the wall behind the green before disappearing out of bounds. Just short in two himself, he then chipped close enough to force another concession. Two up after five. Tiger looked frustrated, uncomfortable and decidedly rattled but Gary chose to keep his feet and thoughts firmly on the ground: "I'm now flying, but I'm not looking ahead thinking I'm going to win this game. I'm only looking at the next hole and the next shot."

This proved good self-advice when Gary was handed a stark reminder of Tiger's ability at the short par-3 7th. With his own ball already safely on the putting surface, Gary watched as Tiger's wedge shot appeared to be heading through the green once more. But this time the ball pitched on the back edge and fizzed back 40 feet towards the hole. It only produced a half, but for Gary it was a timely reminder that Tiger was capable of shots that he couldn't even contemplate.

Tiger's length helped him claw one back at the par-5 8th, and a good up and down on the 9th kept him just one behind. On the 10th Tiger was again through the back, but played a 'delicious chip', in Gary's word, to save the hole. Even so, Gary was becoming more certain by the minute that Tiger's invincibility had been overstated. He remembers thinking: "If he keeps making mistakes, I'm going to win this match because I'm more in control of my game than he is of his." Back on the 5th hole Gary had joked with Colin about Tiger's length: "I'm used to people out-driving me, but this is taking the Mickey!" When Colin replied, "he is long, isn't he?" Gary's retort was, "yes, but length isn't everything, is it?" Again, the potentially demoralising effect of Tiger's power golf was being neutralised because the rest of his game was punctuated with errors.

A four-club advantage for Tiger on the par-3 11th only produced another half, but by the time they arrived at the 14th, the match was back to all square. The 14th is a 152-yard par-3, which proved pivotal to Gary's success that day. Playing first, Tiger went through the back of the green for the umpteenth time and found an awkward spot. Gary was playing for the heart of the green but pushed it just a fraction. The left to right wind toyed briefly with sending his ball into the deep right-hand bunker, but relented and allowed it to land safely on the green just 15 feet from the pin.

Tiger kept his turn when he was unable to coax his chip any closer than 20 feet, but any thoughts Gary might have been entertaining about having two for the hole were banished in an instant as Tiger rammed home the par putt amid much fist-pumping. The TV cameras and crowds were now out in force as other matches had finished and word had spread that Gary was more than holding his own. Distracted briefly by the cameras, Gary had the composure to step away, refocus, and go through his routine again. His putt found the middle of the cup for a timely win. One up, four to play.

An American journalist who had covered much of Tiger's amateur career to date later told Gary that it was the first time he had ever seen a look of doubt on Tiger's face. Gary had also sensed that this was the moment Tiger realised he could lose: "I knew I could win. I knew before – but real belief started to creep in at that stage."

In an ideal world, a golf course would not now present you with a 467-yard par-4 into the teeth of the wind, against an opponent who can hit it into the next county. However, that was exactly what Gary now faced, but he had known from early on that this would be the toughest hole since the 3rd so refused to allow this to faze him. Holding this realistic outlook made it easier to accept when his 5-wood approach came up short and Tiger's 8-iron found the heart of the green to set up a two-putt win. Back to all square.

A 278-yard carry is required to clear the cross-bunkers on the 16th so most sensible golfers wouldn't even have considered it back in 1995. Tiger wasn't interested in sensible golf at this point and made his intentions clear by pulling out the driver. Convinced that Tiger hadn't struck it properly, Gary could only watch in amazement as the ball rejoined terra firma safely over the waiting bunkers. He had cleared them with a mishit! Gary's own mishit tee shot and miscalculated second had left him 30 yards short still in two, but fortunately for him Tiger failed to capitalise by hitting his 9-iron approach through the back into a poor lie.

Gary accepted the reprieve gratefully, pitching nicely to leave himself 'one of those putts' as Peter Alliss might well have been saying in the commentary box. Tiger's chip was a mediocre effort, but again he holed the putt to leave Gary staring at a 'must-make' 6-footer. Despite hitting a poor putt, Gary was delighted to see the ball find its way home out of "pure determination" as he later put it. Perhaps fate was on his side. Certainly the crowd was. Was he now destined to win? These thoughts briefly crossed his mind as he rode the crest of a confidence wave to the 17th tee, fuelled by the enthusiastic home support.

Gary's best tee shot of the day on the par-5 17th meant that despite being 50 yards short of Tiger, he could also get home in two. His crisply struck 5-wood rolled just through the back, where it was joined moments later by Tiger's approach. The tit-for-tat continued on the chips with Tiger now inside Gary's ball by about a foot, but certainly not dead. At this point Gary suffered what golfers fatalistically have to accept as payback time. Whereas his poorly struck putt on 16 had found the bottom of the cup, his perfectly struck putt here somehow contrived to stay above ground. Gary couldn't believe it: "For the life of me I don't know how it didn't go in." His anguish quickly gave way to the blunt realisation that Tiger now had a 4½ footer to win the hole and go dormie one up. But not only did Tiger's drilled attempt lip out – it also went nearly as far past again. To his credit he made no mistake with the return, and they walked to the final tee still locked together at all square.

The 413-yard 18th hole plays directly back towards the sea, which by this time was bathed in a carpet of gold from the setting sun. Tiger opted for his 1-iron to avoid running out of fairway, but turned it over slightly into the left hand semi-rough. Gary's drive safely found the right-hand side of the fairway just 15 yards behind Tiger.

As Gary and Colin descended the hill, they were struck by the sheer size of a crowd some seven to eight thousand strong. But by the time they reached Gary's ball, they were focusing only on getting the yardage right. There were no prizes for going right where the only really severe rough on the entire course lay in wait, but equally anything leaking left risked going out of bounds into the clubhouse surrounds. The shot was really a 3-iron or perhaps a 4-iron running in, but Gary opted for percentage golf. He explains: "I decided to hit 5-wood, because at that stage I was not comfortable with my striking because it was soft squidgy turf and I didn't want to fat an iron. 5-wood was the safe shot."

The ball finished just off the green to the right, safely avoiding the dreaded thick stuff. Gary and Colin were standing just 40 yards ahead of Tiger when his

7-iron approach set off, but Tiger's early lean hinted that something was badly wrong. It was. His ball cleared the crowd on the left and disappeared, leaving Colin uttering in disbelief: "He's gone out of bounds!" Despite realising what this could mean, Gary's thoughts remained clear and rational: "I can't afford to think about whether he's out of bounds or not. I've got to get to my ball and make a four. If I make four then he can't win the hole, unless he holes his second ball. So that was all I was thinking about – making a four."

There was turmoil around the green, but eventually the signal reached Tiger up on the hill that he had indeed gone out of bounds. His second ball landed with a thud 15 feet above the hole. He could still salvage a five, but it would be a tricky putt.

Gary had known from a few holes back that a win was likely to put GB&I two ahead going into Sunday's second phase of matches. Perhaps that had contributed to some slightly 'steery' golf over the closing holes, but now all that mattered was this next chip shot. The lie wasn't great so it demanded his full attention, but Gary followed his pre-shot routine to the letter and executed a perfect chip to about 2½ feet. The crowd roared its approval. More importantly to Gary, he hadn't buckled under the weight of his team's hopes. Moments later, Tiger's last gasp attempt slid by, and he moved quickly across to look Gary in the eye, shake his hand and say, "thanks for the game."

For a moment, Gary felt sorry for Tiger, empathising with how he would be feeling if the roles were reversed. But this quickly gave way to elation and gratification as team-mates, interviewers and mum rushed in. Gary remembers just what that moment meant to him: "All of a sudden I truly felt justified to have been selected."

It was storybook stuff indeed – Gary had struck a huge psychological blow by slaying America's Goliath on his Walker Cup debut, his win had put the team two ahead and spelt out that victory was a realistic possibility and ultimately it helped pave the way for GB&I's first Walker Cup triumph on home soil for 24 years.

Gary's celebrations had to be relatively short-lived as there was still a lot of golf to be played the next day. But this wasn't a huge issue since one of his strengths has always been to sail an even emotional keel rather than the choppier waters of pronounced highs and lows. In fact, while some of his team-mates were so drained when it was all over the following night that they wanted no real part in the forthcoming Home Internationals, Gary felt he would always be ready to play the next day even if he'd just lifted the old Claret Jug!

Pressure – it's all about perception

Gary's outlook was that, "there's always tomorrow, the next hole, the next match, the next tournament." Yes, he wanted to win with a passion – but golf wasn't, and isn't, life and death. While others proclaimed this was his greatest achievement, he preferred to think of it as a very special moment, but ultimately just another game of golf. With Gary's philosophy it's easier to escape the ravages of pressure that can afflict golfers so adversely. Gary sums it up this way: "Pressure is not a physical thing. It's a created thing. Your own mind creates pressure – nobody else does. They can help to create it, but the only person who truly creates the pressure you're feeling is you yourself. If you analyse it and study it rationally, often there is really little to fear!"

Like David all those years ago, Gary had been able to paint a picture in his mind in which his background and strengths might prove of more value than Tiger's Goliath-like power-hitting. Despite his opponent's formidable record, Gary was the older and more established player with a wealth of experience dating back to his county debut in 1982. He was certainly far more accustomed to links golf and the conditions they encountered that day. He also knew there were no guaranteed winners in golf. Everyone was beatable, even the mighty

Tiger who confirmed just how good he was a mere 18 months or so later when he won The Masters by a record 12 shots.

Just play your own game

In answer to any questions about the key psychological weapons that helped him achieve his famous victory, Gary's response is this: "It was definitely that I stayed in the present and that I had the confidence in my own ability. I was playing my own game. I just literally played the golf course. I didn't play the individual because I couldn't outplay my opponent blow for blow… it wasn't possible. I just had to stay in the present and play my own game." He also knew that he could use any nervous energy the prospects of his match had generated to his advantage by channelling the resulting adrenaline in a positive direction. Where negative nerves can paralyse performance, positive nerves can lead to a sense of excitement and anticipation and actually enhance performance.

Then there was the golf course. Learning to love the venue is a policy advocated by Peter McEvoy. While you cannot change the golf course itself, you can fall in love with the competitive opportunity it presents, even when you feel it doesn't particularly suit your game or play to your strengths. There is possibly even more satisfaction to be had from playing well in adverse situations such as this. So although Gary had felt Royal Porthcawl didn't particularly suit his game, he managed to find reasons why the conditions and test it presented might actually suit him better than Tiger. Top American sports psychologist, Dr Bob Rotella, tells the story of how Gary Player used to exasperate his fellow pros by claiming to love slow greens one week and fast ones the next. When pressed to clarify which ones he really preferred, Player replied: "You just have to love whatever greens you're playing on!" There is absolutely no point being negative about a venue you may have to play one day – you'll be so weighed down by pessimistic thoughts, you might as well not bother putting your clubs in the car.

Perhaps the one crucial lesson to be learned from Gary's magnificent Tiger-taming performance is this – stay in the present. The past? It's gone – you can do nothing about it. The future? You can't deal with that until you get there. But as for the present? We'll let Gary explain why that's the most important place to be on the golf course: "The only thing you've really got to worry about is the shot you've got to play next. It's the only thing that matters at all. Each shot is its own challenge, separate to anything else. You play one shot at a time. If you treat each shot as a separate entity I guarantee that you'll have a truly great golfer in the making – particularly if they also have a good measure of ability and aptitude for the game."

No one is invincible. Every Goliath can be beaten!

A never-ending story

Matt Richardson

When Matt Richardson reached the very pinnacle of English amateur golf at just 19 years of age he could well have been tempted to think, 'that's it, I've cracked it.' Fortunately for his long-term golfing prospects, he has chosen to see success as more of an ongoing process in which he'll always be striving to look forwards rather than backwards, and in which sound mental preparation plays a key underlying role.

"I think what separates me is that if I win – for example, the European Amateur championship, qualifying for The Open as a result – before I've landed home I've already forgotten about it. I've swallowed it and I'm ready to get myself started on my next step. That's the thing that's amazing to me. You win something and you think, 'that's no big deal' and you move on. That's my attitude."

Once the years of secondary school education are over, those destined for success at the very top level of most professions usually face a very long journey demanding abundant hard work, sacrifice and dedication. The legal and medical professions spring readily to mind.

Sport is one of the rare arenas in which success can be available at a much earlier age for those who possess the necessary raw talent. But often, particularly with individual sports, it can take years for the mental game to catch up with the physical one. There are exceptions such as Boris Becker who burst so miraculously onto the tennis stage back in the mid-1980s and more recently, Roger Federer, who has shown the same characteristics as Becker in his rapid rise to world tennis domination. But in golf, mental inexperience can often temporarily, and sometimes permanently, prove a real stumbling block in a player's progress towards fulfilling their potential. There are plenty of youngsters who hit the ball seemingly well enough to achieve anything. But for many of them, the relative immaturity of their golfing minds can be the key thing that holds them back. Mental progress is often at a slower rate to technical progress.

Every once in a while though, certain youngsters are able to combine raw talent with mental awareness beyond their years. Then there is no limit to what they can achieve. The Buckinghamshire Golf Club's Matt Richardson is one such example. Matt lifted the Middlesex U-18 and U-21 championships in the same year – at just 14 years of age – before rising rapidly through amateur golf's ranks to top the English Golf Union's Order of Merit while still a teenager. In 2004, victories in the Brabazon Trophy (the English Open Amateur Strokeplay championship) and the International European Amateur championship, along with a host of other strong showings, hoisted him to the very top of English amateur golf.

One of the things that enabled Matt to take his golf to such a high level at such a young age was an early awareness of the importance of golf's psychological side, and a straightforward and efficient application of himself to psychological principles to help prevent his mind undermining his technical promise. Matt says: "I think psychology is massive when it comes to sport. I think if the brain is that strong then obviously it's the key weapon in any sport. It doesn't matter what you do with your hands or your body. For me, the brain is definitely the thing that I've worked on the hardest."

We spoke to Matt about the mental side to success at the end of 2004, as he was looking forward to another amateur year in 2005 that would include a Walker Cup debut in America, and a berth in the Open Championship at St

Andrews courtesy of 2004's European Amateur title. Great Britain and Ireland subsequently went on to narrowly miss out in the Walker Cup that year, but Matt did make the cut at the 2005 Open – one of the highlights of his career to date.

Equipping yourself for the future

Matt believes that tasting victory at whatever standard is perfect preparation for the next level, citing the boost he received from his McEvoy Trophy (English U-18s strokeplay championship) success in 2002, and World Boys Championship crown in Japan later that year. Earning the title of 'best in the world' is undoubtedly a phenomenal confidence-booster whatever the age group.

He was 17 at the time, and thinks an element of semi-ignorance as to where he stood on the world stage may have helped in Japan. As Matt explains: "I went out to the World Boys with no expectations of what world class performance was at the level I was at (i.e. junior level). I went there not knowing what to expect and just played golf. And it turns out I was good enough to be world number one at the time. So I was kind of surprised." The beauty of this seemingly naïve approach was that Matt didn't know where he stood, so had no reason to set his expectations either unrealistically high or unnecessarily low. It was simply a voyage of discovery to find out how good he really was with no added pressure.

Of course, the knowledge he was the best boy golfer in the world would later equip him to approach future events from a very different perspective. By the time Matt found himself travelling to the Eisenhower Trophy (a three-man team event) with Gary Wolstenholme and James Heath at the end of an excellent 2004, expectation levels were understandably higher, but still grounded in the knowledge that he was good enough to justify them. Just before that event Matt's feelings were: "I'm going and I'm thinking 'maybe I can take it home.'

I'm not going to sit here and say I'm thinking, 'I can't do it,' because otherwise I wouldn't come. The priority for me is to win the individual. That's all I can do to help the team. So I'm going to prepare like James and Gary, who I'm sure are thinking 'we're here as a team,' but will also be thinking 'selfishly' as individuals about coming here and winning. It's the only way we can think." When you know what you're capable of, it's fine – within reason – to up the ante as long as you take care not to overburden yourself with expectation. By the time of the Eisenhower Trophy – in which the England squad would subsequently go on to finish 8th out of 65 teams – Matt knew he was good enough to compete on that particular stage. Success at any level should breed enhanced confidence for the next.

Use winter wisely

Throughout Matt's amateur career, planning and preparation have played key roles as he has increasingly sought to map out the path ahead. Winter planning in particular has played a major role – sitting down in the off-season and trying to come up with the best strategies for further success the following year. In winter 2001, when Matt was eyeing the 2002 World Boys Championship in Japan, he devoted the winter months to devising a specifically targeted programme that would optimise his chances of selection. Matt takes up the story: "I wanted to play in the World Boys, so spent my winter figuring out the best angles I could work on and what tournaments I needed to peak for. I decided to go out to Spain for a month and practise. And it worked out that the McEvoy Trophy was where I needed to make my impact to get in the team. So I basically spent the winter thinking about the McEvoy Trophy and hitting specific shots for that in practice."

Whatever level your golf is at, winter is the perfect time to sit down and work out what you'd like to achieve the following season. Most of the big competitions at your golf club will be from spring to autumn, course conditions in winter will probably not be conducive to your best golf, and it's generally a slower time of year – in fact, the perfect time to take stock, look ahead to where you'd like your game to be, and decide on the best way to enhance your chances of making it happen. For Matt, winter will always be a critical time for doing just that in conjunction with his coach: "We sit down and I say, 'right, I've played a couple of tournaments this year where I've felt tired and got this shot, and other times where I wasn't feeling too great, didn't play my best and had this bad shot.' Then we try and find the reasons why I've done things like that. Weaknesses and strengths – you basically need to find out why. There are lots of questions. But I think they're always questions that you can answer."

There has been much talk of the way players like Nick Faldo in his prime, and Tiger Woods now, have tried to focus on golf's four majors, seeking to peak physically and mentally at just the right time to give themselves the best chance of landing the big titles they desperately crave. Matt knows all about trying to peak at just the right time, relating the frustrations of having a game fired up and ready to go in the run-up to December 2004's Eisenhower Trophy, but nothing else to play in. As he prepared to fly to Puerto Rico, Matt reflected: "I've had a month where I've not had anything to play in and yet I've been ready for tournament golf throughout that whole month. So I've almost had to relax and 'lose' the standard of my golf to then re-peak for this tournament. But once I've finished this tournament, it will be everything laid out on the table, get the blueprint out again, look at where I haven't improved enough from last winter, then get cracking on those things and find new things that I need to develop." Any golfer looking for year-on-year improvement would do well to devote the off-season to forward planning.

One of Matt's 2001 winter goals was to be selected for the 2002 World Boys in Japan, and he believed a good performance in the McEvoy Trophy would make that eventuality much more likely. When that carefully tailored plan came together, with victory virtually securing his seat on the flight to Japan, it must have felt good – with the subsequent victory in Japan then providing some very sweet icing on the cake. Something he'd started planning for months earlier had come to ultimate fruition, which was not only very satisfying, but also gave Matt the tremendous mental boost of leaving junior golf at the very top: "I just wanted to dominate my final junior year, and go into men's golf as the guy that had to be beaten. I think that was massive for me. You need to come away with some sort of satisfaction that you've left the stage you're at, at the top. That's what you want to do as an amateur too – leave the amateur scene at the top of your game when you're moving up to pro level so you can justify the fact that you're turning pro." Matt made that transition into the professional ranks after taking part in the 2005 Walker Cup – the ultimate team accolade for amateurs – where he acquitted himself very well, winning both his singles matches comfortably.

Adapting to new golfing situations

But that didn't mean he'd finally arrived. Far from it. Matt is only too aware that it was just another step on a journey that will never end as long as ambition is still burning fiercely. Turning pro was most definitely not the end of Matt's journey, but rather just the beginning of its next leg – one that at the time of writing is proving quite a testing one. After playing just a handful of Challenge Tour and European Tour events in 2006 with limited success, Matt did then successfully play his way through the 2006 tour qualifying school. But 2007 then proved a highly frustrating year in terms of results.

This all means that Matt faces yet more work and planning to help him find his feet and start progressing once again in his new golfing habitat. But that is something he has grown to accept as it's become apparent that golf will be his life's focal point for a long time to come. He says: "One day it just clicked that I'm always going to be working on my technique or doing something. I'm always going to be working. There's not going to be six months of working hard, three months of playing and three months of doing nothing. It's going to be 20/80, where 20% of the time you're playing golf and the other 80% you're preparing in some way or another – for your next tournament or through winter for your next season."

This frame of mind is essential to avoid the complacency that can so easily set in once a particular mission has been accomplished. Matt is painfully aware of the dangers of living in the past having suffered a poor spell of form by his standards immediately after his biggest triumph to date in 2004's Brabazon Trophy: "A lot of people talk about the past. I found myself living in the past for a month or so after the Brabazon which didn't help my golf. It had been a long time since I'd won anything, and it was the first full men's amateur event I'd won. If I look back, I didn't play very good golf the month after because I was still living in the past. What I think normally separates me is that regardless of how big a feat I feel I've achieved, I seem to move on very quickly to think about my next project or goal." So later on that year, when he added the European Amateur title to his CV, Matt was careful not to fall into the same trap. As you've read in this chapter's opening quote, his reaction then was much more along the lines of, 'yes, that's a great achievement; now what's next?'

You may need to rethink things

Now Matt has joined the professional ranks, he's aware there may be implications with regard to his level of practice. He may have been a full-time amateur for several years, but recognises that playing for money and aspiring to reach the pinnacle of the game may – or may not – demand an increased workload: "Self-admittedly I think my work ethic is probably 30-40% compared with that of players like Padraig Harrington or Vijay Singh. But I'm 22. I only played golf for seven or eight years as a 'professional amateur' – and only developed seriously in the last five years. There were only really five or so years where I was really trying to figure out how I do things. So I think I'm always going to be learning with respect to what's the best way for me to practise.

Right now I could say 'I don't know.' I'm still testing, still finding ways to do things." He's still in the middle of a never-ending learning curve.

He's certainly more Monty than Vijay when it comes to practice. Matt explains: "When I was a junior I never used to like practising, and admittedly still don't like standing there for five hours hitting balls. I find it very hard to concentrate for that period of time. People argue that I can concentrate for four hours on the golf course. But it's not like that. You hit a shot, then walk in between shots, so you've got time to switch on and off. Four or five hours hitting balls is intense mental pressure for me." But that's not the end of the story, as he continues: "As I say, I probably do 30-40% of a top workaholic on the European Tour. But that's the standard I'm looking to play ultimately, so whether I need to practise like that or not I'll soon find out. But I'll need to find out for myself what's the best way to practise. Maybe I'm a Montgomerie who likes hitting a hundred and fifty balls and playing eighteen holes of golf, rather than standing there and hitting balls for six hours." You get the impression that Matt very much hopes that will prove the case – it didn't do Monty much harm in his Order of Merit-topping heyday. But equally you feel that here is a young man open to the distinct possibility that if he wants to get to the top he may have to intensify his practice regime – and more importantly, that he would be willing and keen to do just that should it prove essential.

That's a lesson for us all. Sometimes we're all too ready to moan that we aren't making the progress we'd like with our golf, when the plain, but undesirable truth, is that we simply haven't been prepared to put in the effort needed to allow that. A sudden plateauing-out frustrates us after a prolonged period of improvement. But that plateau probably represents the boundary of our capabilities based on our current workload. To experience further progress we have to be willing to do more. Often, we're unwilling, or unable to do that, in which case it would be far better for our mental state just to accept that, and only start expecting more if our motivation or circumstances allow us to increase our effort. For Matt, you feel that won't be a problem – much as he may hope his current work ethic will be enough, if that doesn't prove to be the case he won't hesitate to change it.

Using your mind's eye to your advantage

So far we've looked at Matt's attitudes to preparation. What about other key mental skills he uses to strengthen his on-course performance? Matt is a great believer in the power of visualisation – especially the kind where you envisage yourself in situations in which you may later find yourself, trusting that mental rehearsal will make actual events more comfortable and less intimidating when they happen.

Prior to the 2002 season, Matt spent part of the winter visualising specific things about the McEvoy Trophy, an event he felt he needed to peak for to boost his chance of making the World Boys: "I was building scenarios in my mind like the last shot in to the 18th, or the putt to win, or the 1st tee shot – things like that. And also sort of picturing myself winning the tournament." Could that not simply be construed as wishful thinking? Not as far as Matt is concerned. For him visualisation is about preparing mind and body for events to come, because at its most powerful it can actually convince your body something has already happened, providing you with 'experience' of a situation you haven't experienced: "One of the keys to my success is the visualising I do because I'm almost conning myself in to thinking and believing I can do something if I visualise it happening. People say that sometimes your mind can be strong enough. In a deep sleep or coma you can be dreaming of something happening and it can be so real that your mind can convince your body that it is actually happening." Powerful visualisation can provoke the same feelings and responses as real events.

The process of success

As we've seen earlier, Matt is not going to be one to rest on his laurels after any achievement, especially after that brief downturn in performance following the Brabazon Trophy. For the foreseeable future and well beyond, success for Matt will be an ongoing process. Matt recognises it has to be this way if he is to achieve what he hopes to achieve: "I think there's a process of success. There's the planning, preparing, and sacrifice and then I suppose what you would call the execution and whether or not it does bring success. That's the process. But when you achieve something there's another process in that you realise what you've done, accept it, and move on. I think the people at the top are the ones who do that the quickest, because they're hungry for more."

Good players know their method of success, and when they win they also know why they've won and what they need to do to have a chance of winning again. And with standards in golf getting better all the time, and far more players capable of putting good scores together than perhaps in previous eras, what they need to do to keep up with the best is keep improving all the time themselves too. And beyond good there's always great. In his book, "Good to great", Jim Collins actually goes as far as to describe good as the enemy of great! Why? Because when you're a good performer you're generally comfortable with the way things are, and to go beyond that and become great you have to do things differently, which inevitably disrupts routines and can prove uncomfortable. So it takes further renewed effort and focus to take yourself from good to great.

The moment you think you've arrived is very often the moment you get stuck in reverse. There should always be a next thing to work towards. Matt is probably not even halfway along his particular golfing journey. Yes, at the end of 2004, he'd reached the top of the EGU's amateur order of merit, and in 2005 he played in the Open Championship and the Walker Cup before turning pro. But the journey prior to that had already been a long gradual one – starting out in the game, improving, making a name for himself at club level, winning the club championship, playing well in county events, catching the eye of county selectors, winning a county event, winning the county order of merit, doing well in a top amateur event, attracting the attention of national selectors, winning a top amateur event. Every one a satisfying achievement in itself – but not the end.

Watch the road ahead not the one just travelled

The next steps Matt is hoping to take involve success at tour level and ultimately a win. Beyond that, if Matt's game proves good enough, the potential journey still doesn't stop – another win, a high finish on the Order of Merit, good performances in the majors, the Ryder Cup and perhaps on towards Vijay's or Tiger's levels of achievement. Who knows? And here's the real secret – even then, when the achievements are colossal, they can always be bettered if the desire and ambition is still there. How could Vijay have possibly improved on his 2004 season? Well, perhaps 10 wins instead of nine or another Money List record. How could Tiger improve on his phenomenal record? More majors in his career-long quest to top Jack Nicklaus's total, eclipsing Vijay's 2004 Money List record, or winning every time he tees it up rather than just every other time. Unfeasible? Maybe, but he pretty much achieved just that for a prolonged spell between his Open success at Hoylake in July 2006 and his season-opening victory in the Buick Invitational in January 2007. And on being asked if his game was as good as it could be when victory in the Wachovia Championship in early May 2007 had taken his early season record to three wins out of six, Tiger replied with a laugh, "it's three short of where I wanted to be!" There is always scope for future improvement however great one's achievements to date may be.

Your own process of success will depend on your ability. But whatever the standard of your golf, you should always be able to see a future level of achievement – something you can realistically aspire to beyond your current standard so that perhaps on 31st December each year you can take a look in the mirror and say, 'yes, I am a better player than I was on 1st January.' The steps towards it may be gradual and perhaps imperceptible to the naked eye, but if you've accomplished a goal of, say, getting your handicap down to 14, you can always then try for 13 – chances are you've played to 13 a few times just to get down to 14, so you know it can be done. And then 12, and then 11… or whatever. The crucial thing is to set yourself appropriate, realistic steps towards achieving those goals rather than giant strides that will probably prove beyond you and have the potential to leave you feeling demoralised. Tiger Woods calls these 'baby' steps forward – small, but achievable goals. If you don't continue to push yourself, you'll stagnate, and hopefully you're not yet ready to settle for stagnation.

Matt has achieved an awful lot in golf in a very short space of time – far more than most of us will achieve in a lifetime. But for him that's not enough; that's not the end of it. He's not wasting unnecessary time looking back on his achievements so far – excellent though many of them have been. He's looking forwards to what comes next. And as we've seen – there can always be a 'next', however good or great you've become.

An Owen goal

Greg Owen

In early 2003 English professional, Greg Owen, had become widely regarded as one of the best players on the European Tour never to have won. But midway through that season he was able to recover from the crushing disappointment of another near miss in Portugal and finally make the breakthrough in the British Masters at the Forest of Arden. This chapter traces Greg's seven-week mental turnaround between those two events.

"I thought I'd missed my chance in Portugal, and I was thinking, 'this is never going to happen.' Then in the Benson and Hedges I played the worst I'd ever played, and David Ridley, my coach, sat me down and said 'look, you can't do this, you've got a living to make, you've got to learn from what happened in Portugal and take it forward.' Next week I played in a different frame of mind, finished 8th and it set me off again."

There are two mantles in professional golf with which players do not wish to be adorned for long. The 'best player never to have won a major' tag that Phil Mickelson finally rid himself of at Augusta in 2004, passing it gratefully on to other great players who have never quite got over the major hurdle – perhaps Monty or Sergio Garcia. And the more common title of 'someone who really should have won by now but hasn't.' The latter probably rests on a dozen or so shoulders at any one time – tournament bridesmaids with everything on their CVs except a win.

One such player in 2003 was England's Greg Owen, who from 1995 onwards had been establishing himself first as a good tour player, then as an ever-present in Europe's top 40. Between 2000 and 2002 Greg racked up 16 top-10 finishes – never fewer than five a season – finishing 39th, 32nd and 37th respectively on the Order of Merit. But he still hadn't been able to deliver the maiden tour win that every player strives for, with his best results remaining three 3rd place finishes in 1999, 2000 and 2002.

The 2003 season had started steadily for Greg in some of the tour's far-flung destinations, and he arrived at the Portuguese Open in mid-April on the back of a solid 14th place finish in Qatar. What happened next took him to the very brink of that maiden success, before ultimately ending in a failure that precipitated an unprecedented mental low. At the end of the tournament, Greg recalls: "I came off the course and I was almost in tears... I was devastated and I thought, 'am I ever going to win a tournament?' The following week I probably played the worst I'd ever played. I just wasn't bothered. I didn't want to learn. I wasn't practising. It was only the week after and I was playing terribly."

In fact that terrible spell lasted just two tournaments – the Spanish Open and the Benson and Hedges International Open – producing finishes of 146th and 143rd, which isn't a million miles from last place in a 156-man field two weeks running. Yet just four weeks after that, when the next opportunity to secure that elusive first win came along at the Forest of Arden, Greg had regrouped sufficiently to be able to grab it with both hands and walk off with the British Masters trophy.

So how had he been able to lift himself from his lowest ebb to victory in just seven weeks? We travel the road from Portugal to the Forest of Arden here with Greg to see what went on in his mind between the two events, and learn how he felt his Portuguese experiences left him better equipped for the next time.

First we need to clarify just why that Portuguese failure was such a bitter pill for Greg to swallow. Events had conspired that week to make Greg believe it was 'his turn'. There's a fine line between positive thinking and over-expectation, but when the latter goes unchecked, the fall from such a height brings you back to earth with an even bigger bump. It was a tournament that he'd come close in before, and one that he'd arrived at in a good frame of mind: "I arrived feeling pretty confident then played really well in the pro-am. I thought the course was playing okay and felt very comfortable. I turned up on Thursday, looked at the scores and saw that three-under was leading, and I thought 'this course isn't that difficult.'"

Greg and playing partner Fredrik Jacobson then set about proving that very point in the afternoon by shooting 66 and 64 respectively, distancing themselves from the rest of the field by three shots. Greg remembers, "I came in after the round and thought I'd played okay and just couldn't understand why the scoring was so bad." By the time he'd added a second round 70 to lead by three, the thoughts that this could be 'his week' had become stronger than ever before. Greg later reflected. "I was playing well; everybody else didn't seem to be playing that well. I was getting the scores, playing nicely and feeling 'this is my tournament.'" As he moved into the weekend at the head of affairs Greg remembers beginning to feel more under pressure: "I wasn't nervous, or anything like that. I was more anxious. I felt 'this is my week; if I don't take it now, I'm never going to take it.' It was a different kind of pressure." One that he'd allowed to increase in line with his expectations.

The next day he breezed through the front nine in one-under to find himself five or six shots clear. But then things started to unravel. Greg recalls: "I was cruising really. I felt pretty confident, and then I started missing a few fairways. I just started to make silly mistakes, dropping shots here, there and everywhere. I made a double down 14 and I just struggled in." When expectation levels are at an all-time high, any fall can have an even more damaging effect, so as Greg reflected on a 3rd round 76 he was feeling pretty miserable, facing up to yet another wasted chance. Fortunately, help was at hand to at least cast things in a more positive light ahead of Sunday. Greg remembers: "Saturday afternoon cost me because then I started to think 'I need to get those shots back' – you start questioning what's going on. But I had a chat with a friend Saturday night and he said, 'hang on a minute, you're only a shot off the lead. If you got to a tournament and someone said 'would you like to be a shot off the lead on a Saturday night?' you'd say 'yes'.' That got me really upbeat."

Then after a perfect opening drive on Sunday, Greg got perhaps the first incline that it wasn't going to be his day when his well-struck approach flew 10 yards too far and he failed to get up and down: "I really didn't feel as though I'd done anything wrong and yet I'd made a bogey." The opening five holes actually served up everything from eagle to double bogey, all of which added up to par which is where his final round score remained with five to play – still right in the hunt.

The hole that cost Greg most that week was the 481-yard par-4 14th, which he'd played in five-over par for the first three rounds. In an ideal world Greg should have reassessed his strategy for this particular problem hole ahead of the final round, because when it came to Sunday, it was this hole that really got Greg out of the present moment, beginning to prey on his mind well ahead of when it should have done: "I did have a problem with that hole that week and it forced me afterwards to assess what went wrong, because I was thinking about the 14th hole probably from about the 11th. I was getting too far ahead." Despite a good drive he again succumbed to a bogey there on Sunday, but was still right in the thick of it.

So coming to the 71st hole, a first tour win was still very much on the cards. Greg's Portuguese failure and subsequent British Masters success both involved 3-irons on par-5 71st holes – but with very different outcomes. In Portugal, Greg nailed his drive before hitting what he thought was a perfect 3-iron in. But a bad bounce kicked the ball into a bunker from where he failed to get up and down for the birdie he felt he had to make. To rub salt into the wound, Jacobson chipped in for eagle to go two ahead of Greg, which is the way they finished leaving Greg down in 5th place. Not bad – another solid top 10? Far from it! If Greg had been an angler his arms would have been fully outstretched to explain the magnitude of the one he'd let get away this time.

The level of expectation he had heaped upon himself here meant the extent of the downward mental curve was far steeper than anything he'd experienced previously: "It was a massive low which is not usually like me. I normally fluctuate a little between high and low, but never normally really high and really low." He was simply devastated. It was his week, and it hadn't happened. Was it ever going to happen?

In the immediate aftermath, Greg was in no fit mental state to play golf – hence the subsequent pair of abject performances. His failure to finish off the job in what was supposed to be 'his week' sent him into a dramatic mental decline. But it isn't actually failure itself that causes us these mental issues so much as our response to such occasions. It's always better to respond than to react, as when we react, it often brings with it thoughts about future 'shoulds' or 'shouldn'ts' – what psychologists call Negative Automatic Thoughts or NATs! Responding, on the other hand, usually has much more positive overtones and an implied desire to put things right. Fortunately Greg has a very wise coach in David Ridley, and two weeks of watching his man wallow were more than enough for David. So after the Benson and Hedges debacle, it was David who kick-started the revival which would see Greg finally achieve his dream just a few weeks later. David's words helped put things back in perspective. Greg recalls: "He said, 'get with it, Greg. You've got a big tournament ahead of you. You finished 5th. It's not the end of the world. You had a nice cheque. Now wait for your next opportunity.' So in the Deutsche Bank I played with a different frame of mind and tried to think of good things all the time – to just play golf and enjoy it. I finished 8th there and it set me off again."

It often takes an outside party to bring you to your senses, and while you may not have the luxury of a regular coach, you probably do have a wife, husband or at least golfing partner who will tell it to you straight. Not that David was unsympathetic to his pupil's plight – it was just that he realised sooner than his man that dwelling on past failures was not going to help him push on and achieve his goal.

Greg was regrouping rapidly. Free again mentally from the shackles of his Portuguese demise, the new positive outlook had reaped instant dividends with four solid rounds and a very healthy 8th place cheque in the Deutsche Bank. Then at the Wales Open the week before the British Masters, an opening 74 left Greg with much work to do just to make the cut. This was another pivotal moment. Greg and his caddy resolved to adopt a different approach for round two – eliminating mistakes over and above pushing for a score with all its inherent risks. A few quid on the line between the two of them helped too – considering how much they play for each week, it's amazing how a few pounds can still focus the mind of a top pro!

The plan worked. A no-bogey, four-birdie 68 saw him comfortably in for the weekend, before a couple of steady rounds elevated him to 31st place – hardly setting the world alight but doing wonders for Greg's mental state nevertheless. Greg summed up the new mindset: "We just concentrated on getting back to how I used to play – fairways, greens and if you miss the putt, you miss the putt. Just don't make any stupid mistakes. And that was it. I seemed to be more focused on what I needed to do and played sensibly rather than being too aggressive."

Then, just a week later, came Greg's defining moment. Over the first two days at the British Masters, Greg was in control of both mind and game. Consecutive 68s saw him again head the field into the weekend just as in Portugal. And so to Saturday – widely known as 'moving day' in professional golf, but where the only move he'd made in Portugal seven weeks earlier had been backwards. Greg had learned from that experience: "The thoughts came back in a good way because I thought, 'I'm not going to do what I did in Portugal. It hurt me so much I'm not going to go through that again. If I keep focused on playing, I can win. I'm not going to think 'this is my week'.' I'm not going to try and force it because it doesn't work.'" Lesson learnt sufficiently to enable a stress-free 67 on the Saturday, which brought with it a four-shot lead at close of play. And the real secret? An even keel mental strategy, responding equally calmly to bogeys and birdies. Greg recalls of that third round: "I missed a short putt on the 2nd hole – hit a really good putt and it came out. It was my first bogey in a long time and it really didn't bother me because I knew I was hitting good shots. If I hit a bad shot, I thought, 'don't worry about it because you're hitting so many good shots that they're going to overtake the bad ones.' And with that kind of feeling in your mind, well you keep hitting your good shots. So that was the thought I had in my mind all the way through and I shot 67."

This 'take it as it comes' attitude continued into the final round, which Greg entered with a four-shot advantage. Even a snap-hooked drive on the birdieable par-5 3rd, and an equally terrible 5-iron in couldn't shake him from this new mindset. To some it may seem somewhat fatalistic, but in reality it exerts less pressure on the individual than any alternative. Of that hole, Greg remembers: "I ended up with a bogey on a par-5. But it really didn't bother me, whereas in Portugal it would have done. I thought, 'right come on, just play. You're hitting plenty of good shots so don't worry about it.' I don't think I hit another really bad shot the whole round."

This strategy paid off because when playing partner, Ian Poulter, rattled off consecutive red figures from the 6th to the 8th, Greg responded with three birdies of his own without getting carried away: "When Poulter fired three birdies at me I stayed calm. I didn't celebrate the birdies; I just stayed on a very level plain. That was my intention that I wanted to stay level." When Poulter then found trouble on the 12th and 13th, Greg ended up six clear with four to play.

What happened next – bogey, bogey, birdie, bogey – may seem to the outsider to represent a colossal struggle to close the deal, but to Greg it resulted from a strategy carefully planned to ensure he couldn't shoot himself in the foot. More of that later, but for now suffice to say that no-one fired a birdie barrage at him over the closing holes, and even with those bogeys, Greg ran out a three-shot winner to finally seal that maiden success. So let's examine in more depth the key thought processes that saw him home, including his own take on those final four par-less holes.

Something different for the weekend

The Saturday 76 in Portugal had knocked the mental stuffing out of Greg, so he was only too aware he needed to clad himself in a different set of weekend mental armour when the next winning chance presented itself. No forcing things, no over-expectations; just a solid focus on playing each shot as it comes and accepting the results. This Langeresque mindset, in which a spectator stumbling across Greg's match might have been unable to tell if he'd just made birdie or bogey, enabled him to reverse Portugal's Saturday figures – 67 instead of 76; "If I made a bogey I didn't want it to bother me; if I made a birdie I didn't want it to bother me. I think you can see from the TV footage that every time I made a birdie, I just picked the ball up, thanked the fans and walked off. I didn't pump the air or anything. I just tried to stay very calm." So a weekend mindset much more akin to that of the earlier rounds. It had worked well enough to put him at the head of the leader board on Friday and Saturday, so why change it?

This strategy devalues the currency of mishaps so they are just that – mishaps, rather than doom-laden signs of the beginning of the end. When Greg bogeyed the 3rd hole on Sunday, that's all it was in his mind – just a bogey, and not suddenly a reason to start doubting himself or his otherwise good play. His response was simply 'so what, I'm playing well, I can create more chances'. He chose to remain realistic and optimistic, preferring to dismiss that early bogey as just a minor blip rather than a disaster.

Physical symptoms; psychological causes

Greg had a very different attitude in the closing round at the Forest of Arden. In Portugal, self-generated pressure had added to the likelihood of failure, so David Ridley had encouraged Greg to analyse Portugal by all means, take what he could from it to equip himself better for the next time, then just let it go. Ultimately Greg's problem was that too much pressure produced a specific mechanical response: "The trouble with me is that when I start trying to push it, trying to work hard, I tense up and my posture weakens." This is why the mental game is so important – mental mistakes lead to physical errors. The two are inextricably inter-linked. Crooked thinking can't actually play a bad shot – it is the effect that wrong thinking has on physical responses that produces bad shots.

Don't try too hard – let it happen

One of the main things Greg had learned over that seven-week period was that it is definitely possible to try too hard. After his victory Greg was much more aware of this: "You can't determine who wins a tournament. You can only play your best golf and see what happens. At the Forest of Arden, I missed a couple of fairways in the last round and got good lies. Little things go your way and it does make a difference." Good things are much more likely to happen if you just try your best rather than trying desperately to win. Far better to play each shot to the best of your ability, and trust that the results will come. That was certainly the strategy that ultimately brought Greg the win he'd been longing for.

Reading the bounces

It's amazing how differently you perceive 'rub of the green' depending on its outcome. Greg has become much more aware of this as a result of his experiences, and from watching golf on telly in 2004 while recuperating after an operation. He remembers a bad break on the 10th hole of the 3rd round in Portugal where his second shot buried itself in an ice plant to produce the bogey that precipitated his slide down the leader board. Not a bad shot, but harshly treated in his opinion. Conversely, he also remembers shots that came off to perfection at the Forest of Arden from difficult spots, and other occasions where he walked up to his ball in the rough to discover an unexpectedly good lie.

All the golf that Greg watched on TV as he convalesced in early 2004 really brought home to him the extent to which winning can depend on 'rub of the green' – something that is outside the individual golfer's control: "You actually look at some of the leaders and it's amazing how many good bounces they get. They don't really play that well. They hole a few putts and sometimes it comes down to a few breaks at the right time – that's when you've got a chance of winning a golf tournament." This makes it far less prudent to adopt the 'why me?' approach to bad breaks. As Greg points out: "Most people in life see more of the negative side than they do the positive. When you're playing well and keep getting bad bounces it affects you more. If you get good bounces it makes you feel really good; if you get bad bounces it makes you feel really bad – yet you could be playing exactly the same golf. If the bad bounces affect you more, you're going to get more and more down on yourself and eventually start playing worse. You have to reassess." A good way to reassess is to take a more objective view. Both good and bad bounces happen, but thinking 'why do I always get the bad bounces?' serves no useful purpose. It's far better to try and accept the bad ones as part and parcel of the game, while embracing the good ones with greater gratitude. After all, from Greg's observations above, winners apparently get more good bounces!

Home comforts

As a serious golfer, it often helps if you're able to get away from the game when you're not actually playing. So take full advantage when events conspire to afford you a better chance of doing just that. Greg felt that being able to stay in his own house for the British Masters was of significant benefit. He could go home, switch off, and play with his daughter rather than beat himself up mentally in a solitary hotel room over what went wrong as he'd perhaps done in Portugal. Staying in the same complex as other players makes it harder to get away from golf-talk, and easier to dwell too long on what's just happened or what tomorrow may bring. That's a long time to think about things that you really can't influence until you tee it up the following day. So it's worth exploiting 'home' advantage whenever it presents itself – in fact, shrewd golf punters read the 'place of residence' details in a player's tour biography very carefully. As Greg comments: "I was more comfortable staying at home. You get away from the golf and it feels more like you've gone out, played a round of golf with your mates and gone home... I try and keep myself to myself quite a lot on tour, but it's a lot easier if you're just coming home." And if – as will more often be the case – you don't have the luxury of being able to stay at home during a tournament, you can still take certain steps to make things feel more familiar. For example, Jack Nicklaus famously used to travel with his own pillow, while Sven-Goran Eriksson arranged for box-loads of Jaffa cakes to be shipped out to the England team's hotel during the Japan/Korea World Cup in 2002.

Positive distractions

It's impossible to concentrate non-stop for four or five hours at a time, and the best results come when you switch your focus on and off as required. That's easier said than done, but still achievable if you can find something else to deliberately occupy your thoughts during any downtime. For Greg that meant thinking about his then one-year-old daughter, Lauren. Distractions can ensure those five of six minutes between shots are spent on happy thoughts rather than agonising over what's just gone wrong or what you've now left yourself. Besides, it might not be as bad as you imagine when you actually get to your ball, so why spend five minutes in a potentially unnecessary negative frame of mind which can be difficult to snap out of?

At the British Masters, this strategy really helped Greg stay in the present better than he had done in Portugal: "I had a determination not to look ahead of myself as I'd done before. If ever I came to a hole and I was thinking about something else, all I tried to focus on was my daughter. I got completely out of thinking about winning, so I wasn't using up too much energy thinking about golf. I looked at the ball, then thought about the shot, and then if I needed to I just went straight on to think about my daughter. People say 'just play one shot at a time', but that was probably about the first time I'd ever really done it. Once I got to the ball, I stopped thinking about my daughter and I'd think about the shot. It's amazing how you think you do it before, but until you've really got into that zone…" Keep your mind pre-occupied and it's less likely to jump up and bite you. Quite a good technique to try out on the course is the 'funnel approach' to concentration. Once you have hit your shot off the tee it can often be difficult to see exactly what sort of lie you've left yourself. Since there's nothing you can do about it anyway, you might as well take a break from concentrating for the majority of the long walk down, and then as you funnel in on the ball over perhaps the last 20 yards or so, switch the concentration back on once you've got a clearer idea about the next shot you face. If you concentrate all the time, your mind goes mad with imagined lies and potential problems which aren't even visible off the tee and may prove totally unfounded.

Do what you have to do

After Poulter had bogeyed 12 and 13, Greg realised that a big lead meant no need for any heroics down the stretch – especially with two tough par-3s and two water holes to negotiate. So rather than being needlessly aggressive he played sensible shots that took big numbers out of the equation: "The fact that I had a six-shot lead with four holes to play meant that I just played more conservatively and didn't mind about the odd dropped shot, because I'm not going to make a double. Three bogeys didn't bother me at all. You do what needs to be done. What's the point in trying to make a birdie on every hole? You play the percentages. The only way I had a chance of losing was if I kept hitting it in the water. So I kept clear of the water."

As Greg says, just do what you have to do and make bogey your worst score. For example, he hit a good shot on the tough par-3 15th that just went a fraction too far. But he made sure he missed the green where bogey was the worst he could do. There's no satisfaction in going down in a blaze of glory, even if it does make good bar talk or keep the press happy. Mr Van de Velde may one day decide he could perhaps have taken a more prudent option standing over his approach to the 72nd hole at Carnoustie in the 1999 Open Championship. To finish 1st, you first have to finish — or finish safely in some cases.

Thanks for the memory

So why in the middle of this conservative game plan did Greg then take on a 200+ yard shot over water into the par-5 17th? Again, Greg has a logical answer: "I hit a really good drive down the middle and sometimes that can be a bad thing because it forces you to decide, 'do I take this shot on or not?' We got down there and looked at the yardage, and it wasn't a case of being in between clubs. So I thought, 'just pick a shot and hit it'. You just turn your concentration up that little bit extra, and I hit it absolutely perfectly and made birdie there." Others were less sure as Greg recalls: "I heard Darren Clarke was watching it on the monitor and saying, 'I can't believe he's taking it on; what's he doing?' But my way of thinking was 'that's the shot to play. I'm going to play it, and if it doesn't come off, I'll get a drop, play on and make bogey. If I lay up, then spin it in the water, I'm making double or triple.'"

That 3-iron to the green set up the birdie that more or less sealed the title, but more importantly, Greg's decision-making process had considered the potential downside and concluded that it was a shot worth taking on. He was prepared to accept the consequences if it didn't come off, and had worked out logically that even if he had to drop back out of the water, bogey was the worst he was likely to do, which would still leave him with shots in hand. That's not negative thinking so much as clear thinking about the options he faced and the potential outcomes of each. Once he actually got over the ball, he was totally committed to the decision he had made. So how did it feel when the shot came off beautifully?: "Awesome. That's why you practise hitting hundreds and hundreds of balls – all your coaching and all the work you put into your career pays off because when you need to hit it you can." The crucial thing here is that you need to develop the ability to think clearly and rationally about the alternative shots at your disposal in pressure situations and then make the right decision based on your ability, rather than taking on some ridiculously ambitious alternative you've never attempted before, not even in practice.

Not only did that 3-iron shot help Greg secure the win, but it was also something he could store away for future use: "At least I know now that if I need to hit a shot like that again, I can go back into my memory bank and think I can do it. If I'd made par there by laying up, I'd probably have questioned myself a little bit more. So it's got to be a positive if ever it happens again." Golfers talk about logging shots, like the one Greg played here, in the memory bank – one for each club in the bag. When Paul Casey holed in one in the 2006 Ryder Cup with his 4-iron one of the first things he said when interviewed was that that shot was going straight into the memory bank for future recall when needed.

Virtually every golfer can recall a round where things got so bad that they gave up striving, only for everything to suddenly fall into place. For Greg the same kind of thing happened in his mind over a seven-tournament spell in spring

2003. He reached such a low point mentally that in some ways, once he had regrouped, the only way was up. And that meant finally being able to achieve victory just a few weeks later.

Since that day in June 2003, Greg has gone on to make the PGA Tour in America his golfing home, and is in many ways going through all this again as he attempts to secure his first victory in the States. He has come close on several occasions, most memorably in the 2006 Bay Hill Invitational, where a three-putt double bogey from just three feet on the 71st hole while leading, gifted the title to a grateful Rod Pampling. Greg put that down to a concentration lapse perhaps borne out of frustration at missing the three-footer for par that, as it transpired, would have seen him two shots clear with just a hole to play. That result may have left Greg over $500,000 richer but it had the potential to leave him in a similar mental state to how he was immediately after the Portuguese Open in 2003. Unfortunately you can't get it right every time, which is how Greg has thankfully chosen to view that unfortunate incident. And at least he knows from his experiences in 2003 that it is possible to bounce back from such disappointments and emerge a stronger player.

The overriding point to emerge from this chapter is that you must make every effort to ensure that what goes on in your mind has less scope to harm what goes on in your swing, because to a large extent your swing will only ever reap according to what you sow mentally. And Greg's certainly worked better when he sowed the right seeds.

A caddy's perspective

Dave Musgrove

You probably think the two most successful Brits in the majors in the late 20th century were Nick Faldo with six and Sandy Lyle with two. But another name slots neatly between them with four – that of veteran caddy, Dave Musgrove, the man at Lyle's side for both his victories, as well as Seve's in the 1979 Open and Lee Janzen's in the 1998 US Open. So who better to ask about the mental toughness he has observed in the players he's worked for – and about the caddy's role beyond that of mere club carrier?

"Remember what they used to say in the war – 'if everybody does their bit…?' If you listen to old war films and stories that's what everybody says. Everybody should just do what they're supposed to be doing instead of worrying about what everyone else is doing. But you see caddies who aren't used to it and they'll be looking at the score, looking at this, looking at that – you've just got to do what you're supposed to be doing and make sure your man knows what he's doing as well."

When Dave Musgrove took redundancy from Rolls Royce in 1972, little did he know that the caddying road he was about to embark on would see him working alongside names of equal renown in the golfing world. Seve Ballesteros, Sandy Lyle, Tom Watson, Lee Janzen and Scott Hoch are among the top players who have chosen Dave as their right-hand man over the past 30+ years.

According to Dave, who first started caddying over 50 years ago as a boy, there are three key rules for the job. First, "show up, keep up and shut up";

then, ensure fingers are well out of the way when your player puts the club back, as it's often returned with far greater force than that used to extract it; and finally, always have a pen on you to increase your prospects of getting paid by 50%, since the most common player excuses are 'I haven't got a cheque book' and 'I haven't got a pen'.

Humorous observations aside, how much can caddies really help beyond the simple practicality of carrying a bag? Well, in an essentially individual sport, the caddy is the only one allowed at the player's side throughout a competitive round, so effectively becomes a team-mate responsible for encouraging, cajoling, advising and sometimes even administering a little discipline.

This chapter looks at some of the ways caddies can help bring out the best in their players starting with some reflections on Sandy Lyle's 1988 Masters victory, before taking a look at some of the key things Dave has observed in the top players he has carried for over the years.

When Sandy Lyle arrived at Augusta for the 1988 Masters he had just won the Greater Greensboro Open the previous week after a play-off with Ken Green. He'd also won a couple of months earlier in Phoenix, so in what was rapidly becoming a busy and successful season, Dave was understandably keen for him not to overdo things in practice. Dave explains: "He knew the course and he was just trying to save his strength. Augusta's a very hilly course – it never looks it but everyone who goes there for the first time is amazed. So he was trying to conserve his energy. He was playing well enough, he knew the course and there was no need to do more than was necessary."

This energy-saving policy reaped instant dividends when Sandy carried his winning form into the first round. A swirling wind and treacherous greens sent the average score spiralling to 77, and Sandy's opening 71 was only bettered by two players. A masterful 67 on Friday then gave him a two-shot lead at the halfway stage, which actually gave his experienced caddy cause for concern. Dave recalls: "He took the lead on the 9th hole and I remember sitting on the 10th tee thinking, 'oh dear, we've got two and a half days of the week to go.' It's very, very difficult to hold the lead from the 9th hole Friday through to the 12th hole Sunday, which is what he did." Thankfully, when Sandy finally surrendered the lead to Mark Calcavecchia after visiting Rae's Creek on that 12th hole to run up a double bogey, Dave was on hand to coax him through those final six holes.

Taking your mind off it

Dave knew there would be a delay on the tee of the reachable par-5 13th, and that hanging around was the last thing his man needed after losing the lead. So he used this time to help get Sandy in the right frame of mind for the closing stretch. Dave remembers: "I said to him, 'it's nowt to worry about. You've only got one man in front of you and he's a volatile sort of player. He's more nervous than you are.' And I said, 'he's right in front of you, you're watching him, and he knows you're only one behind and he's only one in front. And he knows you're probably playing better than him for the simple reason that you won last week and played with him yesterday.'"

Just when Sandy could easily have allowed himself to wallow in the disappointment of losing the lead, his caddy was on hand to fill his mind with positive affirmation about his ability, his form and the task ahead. It was the same a couple of holes later on the 15th, where Dave knew from experience that there was likely to be another delay – first-hand experience from two years earlier when Sandy had played with Jack Nicklaus as the Golden Bear pieced together his miraculous Masters swansong.

That year, Tom Watson and Tommy Nakajima playing behind Nicklaus and Lyle had had to wait until the crowd noise had died down before they could putt out on the 15th, such were the decibel levels Nicklaus's eagle, birdie exploits on 15 and 16 had generated. Also up on the hill waiting to play into the green was Seve Ballesteros, who had eagled the 13th to take the lead. Dave takes up the story: "Seve was stood there all this time waiting. By the time it came to his turn he must have had three different shots in his head and he dunked it in the middle of the lake. We were walking up 17 and the crowd ran across and shouted, 'Jack, Jack, it's in the water.' So when it came to Sandy in 1988, I knew the wait was coming – not for the same reasons, but because it's a short par-5. When you're last off in the Masters you're always waiting. And I knew it was a big one because it's the last shot over water. When you've led all week, you're on a short par-5 and you've hit a good drive you want to get on with it. You don't want to stand there watching. So I thought I'll get his mind off it and I talked about other things – anything but the shot." As it transpired, Sandy failed to birdie either of those two reachable par-5s. But when he holed a slippery 15-footer for birdie on the 16th, then played one of the most memorable bunker shots of all time on the last to set up another birdie, the Green Jacket was his.

Right words at the right time

The best caddies know their players very well, while the shrewdest players will choose their caddies carefully and make them aware of exactly what is expected of them. One thing that is expected is that the caddy will know whether or not to say anything, and if so, what. And once they've decided something does need to be said, there's no room for half-heartedness – it has to be said with real conviction, as Dave explains: "Oh no, you don't back off other than when you really have to. If you think that you're not doing the right thing then you shouldn't be there. It's no good being frightened. You're either right or wrong. As one of my friends in America says, 'say something – whether you're right or wrong, bloody say something!'" That's a lot easier if you have a good enough relationship with your player to know what he needs to hear and when he needs to hear it. Dave goes on: "Well you've got to know the bloke and also the swing thoughts that they've worked on. So when they're standing there under the influence of golf and they don't know where the hell they are – all the coaching and everything else has gone out of their head – you have to say, 'well, the best thing to do is remember your swing thoughts,' and then tell them what the best swing thoughts are. And you have to pick the right moment."

Dave remembers another incident with Sandy in the second round of the 2004 Scottish Open. Sandy had made a mess of the first six holes, and Dave was contemplating a weekend off as they headed for the 7th tee. Dave explains: "The 7th is a tough hole. You've got to hit a good drive and then it's a really demanding second shot. So he hit this tremendous drive and we got up there and he said 'wow, I wish I'd had that lie on the last hole' because he'd duffed a wedge shot there. Now he's got a 7-iron into a very difficult green, and he said, 'I wish I'd had that lie on the last hole.' And I said,' 'Why?' and he said, 'well, it's a good lie.' And I said, 'so are you going to hit a good shot then?' And he went and stiffed it and then had five birdies over the next 10 holes. So you've got to be there ready for the kill with the right words when they give you the opportunity."

The caddy must stay in control, say only what needs to be said, and not get sucked into everything going on all around so that he can remain a calming influence. Dave thinks he has generally succeeded on that front: "I think I was able to do it a lot, but it is very easy to get carried away. You know, 'someone's had an eagle; what's that noise over there?' You don't want to know that stuff. Arnold Palmer said about The Masters in one of his books that he used to put his visor at an angle so he could see the scores but he couldn't see the names of the people who were chasing him. I said that to Lee Janzen once and he then used to say, 'just tell me if there's something I need to know.' That's what he said on the last day of the US Open in 1998 – well all that week really. He said, 'I'm not going to look at that board, but tell me if you think there's something I really ought to know.'"

Hit the fence or hit the fairway?

Lee Janzen was the reigning US Open champion when Dave first started working with him in 1994, but Dave remembers his mind being anywhere but on his golf – a new baby, a new equipment contract and all the hubbub of being a major champion were distracting him from the task in hand. When Janzen spent much of his practice time at the season-opening Mercedes Championship trying to hit as many balls as possible into the fence at the end of the range, Dave was unimpressed: "When he got on the 1st tee he didn't know what to do – he had no idea what to do. So I said to him, 'can I ask you a question?' and he said, 'what?' And I said, 'where's the fence on the 1st hole?' And then he knew exactly what I meant. In other words, when he got on the 1st tee there was no fence to hit it at – he'd got to hit the bloody fairway. So I said, 'listen, what you've got to do on the range is imagine the holes you're going to be playing rather than just hitting balls into the distance.' That's what he started doing, and finally in June he won a tournament."

But Janzen was also a steely competitor able to make seemingly harsh decisions for the sake of his golf. Dave had seen with Sandy Lyle how having friends and family at majors could be an unhelpful distraction, and remembers Janzen's solution to this dilemma: "For a long time he barred all his family from coming to majors. He wouldn't have them. I remember him saying to me, 'does your wife come to the Masters?' and I said, 'how do you mean?' And he said, 'well I've got a spare ticket – I've barred all my family. I've banned the whole lot of them – what's wrong with that?'"

Dave also reckons Janzen had real presence out on the course. He remembers him coming from miles behind to tie Corey Pavin for the 1995 Kemper Open, and then taking total control of the ensuing play-off: "On the tee Janzen just talked him to death. He wouldn't let Pavin get a word in. Pavin was quite an assertive bloke himself, but Janzen took over the conversation – I don't know whether he intended to or not – and then birdied the hole. That was the fifth time that week he birdied the 18th, which was a tough hole as you can imagine. But he just took the situation on."

The best players take control

What Dave most remembers about his year with Tom Watson was what a well-prepared, consummate professional he was: "The best one to work for – and the toughest – was Tom Watson because as soon as he came out of the clubhouse he was in the office. He'd already know which way the wind was blowing, and what the temperature was going to be. You knew he wasn't pissing about. Everyone wants to be a skiver, don't they? But Tom Watson was very, very strict. He didn't say much so you had to watch him, but I knew that before I started with him."

Dave also admired Watson's practice mentality, which is what had prompted him to point Lee Janzen in the right direction. Dave says of Watson: "When he stood on the range he imagined every hole he'd play and every shot he'd be hitting as he warmed up – he would imagine the holes he would be playing on that course."

Dave also recalls Watson's habit of getting across his dislikes in a positive way, and taking control of situations as a result: "He never said anything bad about anything. Even if he hated something he would always turn it into a positive. You knew the things he didn't like but he would never ever say, 'I don't like that' or 'this is no good.' He would always say it the other way around. I remember working for Janzen after finishing with Watson and the two being paired together. On one hole their balls were the same distance away on the green and Janzen was dithering about over whose putt it was. Tom Watson just went, 'it's your putt.' And afterwards I said to Lee, 'did you notice how positive he was with it? He wasn't in any doubt. He walked up and said, 'it's your putt' and you're not going to argue with him whether it is or it isn't.' That's how channelled he is – whether it's right or wrong it's a positive."

Play how you practise and practise how you play

Ask Dave what it was like caddying for Seve and he has no hesitation in replying: "Impossible. Just impossible." But again, Dave believes Seve was one of those players capable of asserting himself in any situation. Dave explains: "It's about making your presence felt. That's how Seve used to go about things – he made his presence felt all the time." But what Dave remembers perhaps more than anything is the mantra Seve adhered to for his practice sessions. Dave explains: "Seve's motto was, 'play how you practise and practise how you play.' So in a practice round you go through the same things you do in a tournament round." In other words, make your practice regime as indistinguishable as possible from the on-course situations you're likely to face, so that practice and tournament modes blur into one.

Be prepared

Dave stayed on in the States after his time with Sandy Lyle, and one of the players he then caddied for was Scott Hoch. What most struck Dave about Hoch was his meticulous attention to detail: "I caddied for Scott Hoch for quite a time. He was a good player. He used to sit in the locker room at least 40 minutes before his tee time with his shoes ready. And he'd come out with exactly the same routine all the time." That kind of repetition breeds familiarity, comfort and confidence so that when you tee off you know that nothing has been left to chance.

Just do your job... and be decisive!

After all those years caddying for some of golf's biggest names, what does Dave see as the key skills required? It's back to this chapter's opening quote: "You've just got to do your job, your own bit. You've got to watch them – you've got to watch and listen all the time. And when you say something, you've got to say it so they know. When I caddied for Seve he couldn't understand a lot of what I said, but he knew what I meant." And what does he think the players are really looking for in a caddy: "Someone who knows what they're doing. But they want a friend too because the point is, it's a game on your own. They want someone who's sympathetic to them, someone to guide them and calm their nerves, and someone who's going to be reliable."

Most average golfers won't have the luxury of a caddy very often, but if your game does progress to the stage where it becomes more or less essential, what should you be looking for? You must choose carefully to ensure that the one person with the potential to really give you an edge out on the course doesn't end up doing just the opposite by rubbing you up the wrong way with both actions and words. Different players want different things from their caddies. Some want help lining up putts; others don't. Some want to discuss decisions; others just want the facts so they can make the decisions themselves. But the best caddies will be so much more than mere bag carriers. They'll have the knack of being able to say the right thing at the right time, they'll know when to say nothing, and they'll be able to spot when you've started to stray from your set routines and take appropriate action to get you back on track.

And apart from the sheer physical effort of lugging a heavily-laden bag round for five miles, what is the most difficult part of the job? Dave has no hesitation here: "The hardest thing is when they tell you, 'I don't want to do this; I don't want to hit that club.' But that's a negative statement, isn't it? So then you're up against a negative right from the off. Negatives are the hardest things to deal with. When they hit you with a negative you've got to counter it with a very good positive, and you've got to be ready for it. That's the hardest thing." And as we've seen countless times throughout this book, being able to counter negatives with positives is only ever likely to be good for your golf.

A coach's perspective

Pete Cowen

Many top players now regard the mental side of the game as sufficiently important to warrant employing someone over and above their swing coach to specifically help them in that area. But just what level of importance does a top swing coach give golf's mental side? In this chapter we get some insight into just that from Pete Cowen, who teaches many of Europe's finest including Darren Clarke, Lee Westwood, Thomas Björn and Henrik Stenson.

"I like to think of it as a pyramid of learning. You look at those things that you need in a golf swing and put them into the building blocks. I think attitude comes right on top of the pyramid. You can have all the things below that like great technique, great discipline, great hand/eye co-ordination and great balance – but if the attitude's poor it can destroy the lot."

Pete Cowen is one of the most respected, successful and in-demand coaches in golf, with a current client list that reads like a 'who's who' of the European Tour. A good enough golfer to play the tour with moderate success throughout the 1970s and early 1980s, Pete then took on the role of head professional at Lindrick Golf Club near Worksop, where he first began to develop a reputation as an excellent teacher. As demand for his services increased, Pete realised that the Lindrick job would have to go if he were to have the time he needed to teach all his star pupils properly. So in 1997 he made the decision to become a full-time golf coach, enabling him to travel more readily to wherever his clients needed him.

As his reputation continued to grow, so too did the list of top names that came knocking on his door, eager to experience the progress that many players in his stable had already enjoyed. Ryder Cup player and nine-time tour winner, Thomas Björn, sums up Pete's appeal in a quote on his website: "Of all the golf coaches I've met in my life, I've not met anybody that's got as big a knowledge of the game as Pete has." That knowledge has been augmented over the years by stints as Senior Coach to both the English Golf Union and the Yorkshire Golf Union, and more recently as a member of the coaching team at the Golfing Union of Ireland. The fruits of all this success have allowed him to open Golf Academies at both the glamorous-sounding Emirates Club in Dubai, and in the slightly more down-to-earth setting of Rotherham in his native Yorkshire.

Both Academies are staffed by PGA professionals trained to teach Pete's approved methods and philosophies, the core strategies of which are a simplification of those elements of the golf swing that have a tendency to become overcomplicated, and a real focus on the development of key short game skills. Much of the work is technical, and the technical elements of the swing form the lower foundation levels in what Pete calls his 'pyramid of learning'. There'll be more about this later, but in simple terms, Pete feels that without a sound technical foundation, anything above that in the pyramid – like natural balance or hand/eye co-ordination – will never be able to make its full impact. Then, as we've seen in the opening quote, the icing on the cake over and above everything is attitude, and if that element is missing, the building work will never be finished and your pyramid will remain for ever 'pointless'. As Pete says, "if the attitude's poor it can destroy the lot."

Over the next few pages we're going to take a look with Pete at the differences between good and bad attitudes, and get the lowdown on how he seeks to ensure all the technical hard work he undertakes with his pupils doesn't come unseated at that final attitude hurdle.

Don't get bogged down in perfection

This may at first seem a slightly strange thing to say for someone entrusted with improving the games of some of Europe's top golfers, playing for the ultimate prizes in the sport. But Pete firmly believes that the constant pursuit of perfection is ill-advised: "I think players focus too much on their best shots and not enough on improving their worst shots. But their best shot is always going to be their best so if they're judging every shot by their very best, in theory a lot of players are failing all the time because there can only be one very best shot." It's a similar scenario to the one about goal-setting in terms of results – any golfer for whom only victory constitutes success is going to spend an awfully long time dealing with failure. Jack Nicklaus has famously said that if only winning is success, then he failed 95% of the time, while even the all-conquering Tiger's strike rate is only around 20%, meaning he fails 80% of the time. But in the eyes of most analysts these two players are just about as far removed from the concept of failure as any golfer who's ever lived.

Every player who comes to Pete will have hit perfect golf shots at some stage – some more frequently than others. Pete's not really interested in those so much as finding ways to improve consistency, so that the destructive potential of a player's less-than-perfect shots is severely reduced. Pete goes on: "When I talk to players I always say to them first of all, 'what are you trying to achieve?' If you don't know what you're trying to achieve… you look at players and they're trying to achieve this perfect golf swing, this perfect shot all the time. And I keep saying to them, 'unfortunately there isn't a perfect anything.' So what you've got to try and do is reduce the odds at the other end of the golf swing so that your deviation pattern is going to come down and down and down."

In Pete's opinion, enhanced consistency is a better and far more achievable route to improvement than constantly striving for unattainable perfection.

Degrees of success

We've already referred to what Pete calls a 'deviation pattern' and that is a key element of his teaching. Pete explains: "If they don't hit it at the flag or it doesn't hit the flag, some players see themselves as failing, failing, failing. Well I don't see that. I see it as slightly less successful if they've hit it to 10 feet, and then slightly less successful again if they're 20 feet away. But it's still a success. I give them what we call a 'deviation pattern' so that they see themselves succeeding, but succeeding more the closer they get to the target. So instead of it being a negative it's instilling positive thoughts in them."

The idea is that rather than setting yourself goals and targets whose potential outcomes are only ever measured in the black and white terms of either failure or success, you actually allow scope for what might be termed partial success, or degrees of success. And that can leave you feeling much more positive about things.

In Pete's example here, yes, if you hit the flag and the ball goes in you have achieved perfection in the form of a hole-in-one or an eagle. But if you're 10 feet away, then most of the time you'll have an excellent birdie chance, and if you're 20 feet away you'll often have a reasonable birdie chance, so why regard that as failure?

Get your engine purring

Pete likes to think that the golf swing is based around two controlling mechanisms, with the body action being the engine room and the arms effectively acting like a steering wheel. He then raises the question: "How are you going to steer something that's running very, very badly? Not enough players focus on their body action being an automatic movement. If you've got an engine, what do you want it to do? You want it to never miss a beat. Well, what are you doing to try and make that engine work more correctly? And they'll say, 'well I'm working on the plane of the swing.' Yeah, but the plane of the swing is actually a consequence of how good your engine is."

If you've got your golfing engine warmed up and running perfectly before you go out and play you won't need to be constantly tinkering with things out on the course. Pete goes on: "I don't want them on the golf course to be thinking, 'well how do I do it?' I always think that it's got to be automatic." And once that automatic status is fully engrained, Pete feels it is something that the best players can just suddenly switch into when the situation demands it: "The great players can hit the ball poorly on the range and all of sudden they get there on the 1st tee and just switch it on. Tiger is the best at it, there's no doubt about it. He can hit the ball very poorly on the range in his warm-up, but he isn't bothered because he knows as soon as he stands on the 1st tee and flicks the switch he's going to perform." This is because the situation or environment has changed, and along with it all the cues and feedback to which the player is responding. The practice ground will be crammed with people hitting ball after ball into a wide open space, perhaps joking with each other and their caddies or taking calls on their mobiles; the 1st tee will be surrounded by hundreds of fans and involve just three players hitting one all-important ball each towards a highly specific distant target as they get down to the real business – two completely different environments.

But of course automaticity doesn't mean switching off completely from all thought processes while you're out on the course for four hours. It only really applies to shot execution, and at other times the difference between good and great players is often down to how well they think when they have to. For example, Monty reckons that his finely developed course management skills are worth one or two shots a round against certain other players, and that's a big saving over a four-round tournament.

'Toothbrush exercises'
If playing on autopilot is the desired state once you're out on the course, what

steps does it take to get yourself to the stage where you can actually do that? There's no quick fix available to you here – it's all down to hard work and highly disciplined practice until such time as it becomes second nature to you. When it comes to judging how people become expert at something, the role of natural talent tends to be overestimated, while the amount of time you need to spend practising skills is often underestimated. On average it requires 10,000 hours to become great at something, whether in sport, music or any field. This is sometimes known as the 10-year rule, and Gary Player has shrewdly observed, 'you must work very hard to become a natural golfer!' Pete uses this dental analogy to describe just how disciplined you must be and why it's so vital if you're to make progress: "People say that Tiger gets up at four in the morning and goes to the gym. That's his routine – it's like a toothbrush exercise. He knows that unless he brushes his teeth every morning they are going to drop out. So just as everybody gets up and brushes their teeth, that's one of his 'toothbrush exercises' – something he's just got to do. You've probably got to have five or six toothbrush exercises that you have to do every day to instil the great discipline that you need to make you more of an automatic player."

If you're looking to take your golf to the next level can you identify half a dozen or so 'toothbrush exercises' that you need to do in your efforts to improve? If not, why not go away and think about the things you could realistically do to help you become more of an automatic player out on the course.

Mapping out the road ahead

In the days before the miracle of sat-nav, if you were setting out on a journey where you knew where you were starting from and where you were heading for, but didn't actually know how to get there, what's the first thing you would have done before setting off? You'd have sat down with an atlas and worked out the best way of getting from A to B within your chosen parameters – whether that was the fastest route, the most scenic route or whatever.

Your golfing journey is a little like that, in that it requires detailed route planning to get you from where you're at to where you'd like to be. But there is one key difference. As you make progress and improve, the original destination you'd set yourself may no longer be appropriate and you might need to extend it further. Even Tiger doesn't feel he's 'arrived' yet – nor is he ever likely to in his mind. Pete explains it like this: "I always think it's like you're going on a journey. You actually plan your journey – where you're going, how you're going to get there. Let's say I've got to get to Dover. How do I get there? Well, I've got to drive down the M1 first and then so on. But then when I get to Dover am I going to get the ferry over or what? And you plan your way ahead. It's the same with the golf swing. You've got to have a plan and say 'right, it starts here and eventually I hope it finishes there.' But it's the old saying that the road to success is always under construction – you never actually get there but you're always on the way there."

So you need to sit down and decide exactly which motorways, A-roads and minor roads you need to take to make your golfing journey possible. Pete explains: "How do you get on the way? Well, it's about structures. That means that you can then get the best out of yourself. Until I actually structure it properly I don't know what the best anybody can be is. But if they start structuring it properly I'll guarantee they've got more chance of getting the best out of themselves."

As with any project, the more detailed and well-thought out the planning stages are, the more likely the project is to come to fruition without the need for costly and time-consuming U-turns or detours, or those frustrating trips up blind alleys where eventually the only thing you can do is turn back before being able to go forward once more. One way to help guard against this is to focus on quality rather than quantity in your practice. There's a world of difference between mindless drills, where basic exercises are repeated without any specific purpose in mind, and mindful practice, where you strive to achieve challenging and specific goals in a deliberate attempt to improve.

The player-coach relationship

The technical and mental sides of the game are so interwoven that a player's swing coach still has a key role to play when it comes to the mental side, not least because getting someone to improve technically is only ever likely to breed confidence. To kick that process off, the coach must be someone that the player is comfortable to be around. Pete uses this analogy to describe it: "I think coaches are a bit like hairdressers for women. They're comfortable with them. They might not be the best hairdresser, but if you're comfortable with somebody around you, you're more likely to have a better feeling about them. So personalities come through a lot."

The ideal player-coach relationship will be a mutually productive one in which both parties are constantly striving to get the best out of each other as Pete continues: "The players that I coach, they push me to my limit because they say, 'no, come on; you can do better than that.' So they do help you to improve, there's no doubt about it. The player helps the coach to improve and the coach helps the player to improve. So it's a little bit of a two way thing really."

The overriding objective is to generate a confidence knock-on effect, in which confidence in their coach gives players the belief they need to then go out and play with added confidence themselves, as Pete explains: "A player should look for a coach he's got total confidence in. Sometimes I see coaches who've got good information but they don't put it over strongly enough and then you can almost see the player thinking, 'well I'm not sure if this is right or not.' And that's really the coach's lack of confidence. Don't ever doubt yourself. If you've got good information, pass that good information on. If you haven't got good information then you shouldn't be out in the job in any case."

So a coach's key roles can perhaps be summed up as information provider and confidence inspirer, and to do that effectively coaches have to have sufficient belief in what they're saying to provide players with the reassurance they crave. But coaches should never become experimenters, using their pupils as guinea-pigs to test out their latest theories, as Pete explains: "At some stage a player's going to say to you, 'are you sure? I don't know whether we are doing the right thing,' and that's the time you've got to say, 'look, I know we are doing the right thing.' And then their confidence goes up and up and up, there's no doubt about that. But you've got to know that the stuff you do works. I've seen it happen that some coaches are experimenting on their players and that's not fair because these players are playing for their livelihoods. You shouldn't be out there if you're not 100% certain about what you're doing."

And the results of this successful transmission of confidence are there for all to see with regard to Pete's coaching, perhaps best summed up in this quote from John Bickerton on Pete's website: "I'd been on tour 10 years and never won… in the past two years we've been working together we've had two wins." That first win came at the end of 2005 not long after the pair had started working together, and preceded Bickerton's best ever season in 2006 when he finished 2nd in the Spanish Open before clinching the French Open title and ending up in the top 20 on the Order of Merit at the end of the year. Bickerton can see a direct 'cause and effect' link between him starting to work with Pete and securing his first win after eight years of trying, so there is clearly good reason for him to have absolute confidence in the man.

The pyramid of learning

One of the concepts Pete has devised to help pupils understand how all elements of their golf games fit together is his 'pyramid of learning' in which he likens the building of a successful golf game to the construction and shape of a pyramid. We should all be aiming to get as high as possible right up to the very tip of the pyramid, but that tip is only achievable if all the key building blocks needed below it are firmly in place. If any are missing, the whole structure loses some of its strength and potential.

Pete likes building analogies when it comes to how best to construct a golf game: "Well it's the old saying that unless you put the foundations in you can't really build it as high as you want. So the better the foundations, the stronger you can build the walls and the higher you can build them before you put the roof on. It's like having the same foundations as a pyramid. And those foundations could be technical, they could be physical and they could be mental so there are all parts in it. What I try and do with the players is say 'right, these are the foundation stepping stones that you need to get to the top.'" If the foundations are weak, your game will always be much more liable to come crashing down around you when the pressure's on.

As we've seen in the opening quote to this chapter there are many elements needed in the building blocks to the pyramid. At the lower levels that would include things like sound technique or the necessary discipline to practise hard. Then as you work your way up you add in the building blocks that are effectively the finishing touches to make you the complete article. And as Pete has already told us, if the tip of the pyramid which represents your attitude is all wrong, everything else loses its effectiveness and you will never be as good or consistent a player as you could be.

Taking responsibility – the three Rs

Just why is attitude quite so important? Pete refers to the 'three Rs' in answering this one – 'respect for others', 'respect for yourself' and 'taking responsibility' – and believes that if any or all of these are missing from your golfing make-up then all the ability and talent in the world is unlikely to get you to the very top. Pete explains this with reference still to his pyramid of learning: "Attitude still fits on the top. People say, 'what do you mean about attitude?'

and that's when I bring in the three Rs. Your attitude shows whether or not you respect anybody. If you're throwing clubs around, cursing, swearing and doing things like that, you're not respecting yourself, you're not showing any respect to others and you're not going to achieve because your attitude's wrong. People won't take responsibility for their own actions either, which is something that I find amazing really – they're always looking for somebody else to blame."

If we're not guilty of these cardinal attitude crimes ourselves, we will all recognise them in people we've played with, so can probably fully appreciate that the negative impact they can have on performance is more than sufficient to hold otherwise good players back. How often do club throwers or swearers spend so long stewing that you start awarding yourself holes mentally if you're playing against them because you just know they can't perform in that mental state? Yet they can't see it. And many golfers spend entire rounds looking for anyone or anything to blame for their poor performance but the one person who is really responsible for every shot they play. Themselves. Pete finds this total abdication of responsibility completely baffling: "I say that every morning you should look in that mirror and say, 'the only person that's going to make me a great player is the guy that's looking back in the mirror. The rest of the people can help, but the only guy that's really going to make me a great player is the guy looking back at me – the guy who has a shave every morning. He's going to make me a great player.'"

So if a poor attitude is holding you back, remember Pete's three Rs – respect yourself, respect others and take responsibility for your actions.

You won't always get out what you put in

One thing that Pete is also keen to stress is that hard work alone does not guarantee you the results or success you yearn for, and that the game continues to owe you nothing however much effort you put in. At first this may sound a little negative and appear to contradict other advice that to succeed you must be prepared to work hard. But it is actually grounded in reality because the two sides of the equation are not reversible – while you will never succeed as fully as you might without hard work, hard work alone cannot guarantee you success.

Anyone who has ever opened a savings account that's in any way linked to the stock market will be familiar with the phrases, 'past performance is no guarantee of future results' and 'the value of investments may go down as well as up'. They would be good concepts to hold on to with regard to the investment you make in your golf, as while those savings products will have been sold to you on the basis of some generous looking return in the headlines, the bank or building society knows full well they cannot guarantee that you'll get that much back when the policy matures. Perhaps the best thing to do is to keep similar thoughts about potential returns on what you invest in your golf in the small print of your mind, so you're at least aware of it when you set out. Then, if all the effort doesn't ultimately yield the fruit you were hoping for, you'll be able to say philosophically, 'at least I knew there was a chance of that when I started out.'

Pete puts it all into perspective for us here, which is incredibly honest given that the sole intention of his profession is to help people improve their golf: "People actually think, 'I've put so much effort into my golf,' and I say, 'well so did I, but you know it doesn't guarantee you anything.' The game gives you back about 30% of what you deserve or what you put in. If you put a lot in you get 30% of a lot, but you still only get 30% so there's 70% missing; if you put nothing in you get 30% of nothing which is absolutely nothing, so it's all relative and you shouldn't expect it. It doesn't owe you anything. Just because you're prepared to practise 24 hours a day and hit loads of shots, it doesn't give you a divine right to hit every shot straight, every iron shot perfectly or hole every putt, otherwise there would be millions and millions of people out there practising 24 hours a day to become multi-millionaires out on tour!"

To finish this little section in a positive light, sometimes you put a lot of effort in and seem to be getting nothing back – and then, maybe a year or two down the line, it all suddenly clicks and you finally reap the dividends of your labour of love. The game does sometimes have the welcome habit of paying you back when you're least expecting it. Henrik Stenson, one of Pete's star pupils, is a prime example of this kind of delayed reward. Stenson says in a tribute on Pete's website: "Peter is a great coach and he has helped me enormously. He turned my career around when I was struggling. We worked hard for a couple of years without really getting anything. We were going in the right direction, but I wasn't getting the results. I always listen to his advice and he has been there for me and he is one of the best coaches in the world. I owe him a lot."

The results have now been coming in thick and fast for the tall Swede. In 2005 he achieved seven top three finishes and missed just three cuts out of 24 to finish 8th on the European Tour Order of Merit, In 2006 he won twice, had five further top 10s and missed just two cuts out of 23 to move up to 6th. And at the time of writing he was comfortably top of the 2007 Order of Merit after lucrative wins in the WGC – Accenture Match Play and Dubai Desert Classic, and had reached the heady heights of world number six to become Europe's highest ranked player. So rest assured – often all that hard work will pay off handsomely. It's just that sometimes it may take a while. So be patient and keep monitoring improvements rather than merely results as Stenson did throughout this period.

Accept your limitations

If having to accept that all the hard work in the world may not actually yield the results you want is one dose of realism in this chapter, here's another – the sooner you learn to play within your limits, the better player you're likely to be. Pete notes: "Poorer players don't actually take into account what is natural to them. They can actually be much better players if they take notice of what naturally happens to them [when they swing]. I always say a golfer should swing in balance; he shouldn't swing to stay in balance. It's a bit like throwing a ball. You're always in balance when you throw a ball – you don't actually throw yourself off your feet, but I see too many golfers trying to swing outside their own natural balance. So do things that are natural to you. If you're not a long hitter naturally, then don't expect to be a long hitter consistently. Do things that are much more natural to you."

This isn't to say that you shouldn't always be striving to extend the limits of your ability, but rather that out on the course in the middle of a competition is not the time to suddenly try and add a few yards to your drives. If you want to try and do that, explore the possibilities in your practice sessions or lessons. If it's do-able it might involve a lot of hard work or a more radical change to technique than you can realistically commit to or your natural swing can accommodate. If that is the case you'll just have to accept your limitations on that one, and find other areas in which further improvement is possible – perhaps shaving a stroke a round off your putting average. Perhaps the classic example in the golfing context is the player who decides to try and change a safe, reliable fade into a distance-enhancing draw. The problem is that this shot doesn't come naturally to them and what they often end up with is a draw that all too frequently turns into a destructive hook. So rather than being perhaps a few yards back safely down the right side of the fairway, they're rummaging around in the undergrowth on the left looking for a route back out to the short grass. So you must be prepared to accept certain limitations and play to your natural ability and strengths. After all, a natural fade hasn't done Monty too much harm on tour over the past 20 years.

What sets greatness apart

To conclude this chapter with Pete we asked him what he felt it was that separated the great from the merely good. Here's what he told us: "Did Steve Redgrave complain about getting up in the morning, going out on that bloody cold Thames and doing all the training and what have you that helped him win five gold medals? It was his determination to do everything that little bit better, that little bit greater, that little bit more than everybody else. If somebody else got up at 6am it was a case of, 'I'd better get up at 5.30am then.' It was the same thing with Daley Thompson. He said, 'I'd better practise on Christmas Day because my competition might be practising on Christmas Day and come to the point,' he said, 'I'd better practise twice because they might be practising and I just need to be ahead of them.' Ben Hogan had that same mentality. So it's no coincidence that Steve Redgrave, Daley Thompson, Tiger Woods, Ben Hogan and all the top players have got this determination to be the best and are prepared to put the extra in. To these kids that say, 'I don't really like getting up in the morning', I say, 'well alright, but don't expect to be great.'"

And is it possible to tell who's got that extra something just by looking at them? Pete thinks so: "I think all you've got to do is look people in the eye. The eye, to me, tells everything. I can see in a player whether it's the outward confidence that everybody seems to have, or real inward confidence. That's something you actually learn over a long, long period of time. You look them in the eye and you can tell. I don't actually know what it is, but as soon as you look at a player, you know. Sometimes I look at kids and say, 'they're nice players, they look like decent players' but when I last asked the question at an English Golf Union elite squad training session, 'where are you going to be in 10 years' time?', two players stood out and said, 'I know where I'm going to be…' And they were the best two players there by far – they were miles better than anybody else. It's not about bragging rights on their part – it's just purely there, and you can see they actually mean what they say." Motivation plays a big part in developing excellence. A player has to want to do well but must also be able and willing to spend hours not enjoying some of the practice involved, while dealing with boredom and a fairly high degree of apparent failure. This requires enormous patience, and is perhaps what Pete is somehow able to detect when he looks into their eyes.

In Pete's view the defining differences that make someone great rather than just good are the determination, drive and dedication to go the extra mile and leave no stone unturned in their pursuit of success. Pete feels he can even spot who's got what it takes just by looking deeply into their eyes. But what about you and us who, for the most part, are never going to achieve greatness? How would he advise us to go about improving? Pete sums it all up neatly for us here: "If you've got a little bit of discipline and you actually decide what road map you're going to follow and what your routine's going to be, then make sure you keep doing it every day and you will get better – just like brushing your teeth. The unfortunate thing is that you don't always see yourself getting better. You shouldn't always judge yourself by the best. Rather you should be looking to be able to say, 'I can see my bad shots getting better.' Not enough people take enough notice of their bad shots getting better."

Clearly Pete has forged a hugely successful and profitable business out of his undoubted teaching skills, but in talking to the man you genuinely believe his two-word answer to why he does it all, and what he feels perhaps sets him apart from certain other coaches. Those two words? Simply, "I care."